W9-BIR-462

Mable & Gar Hoffman's

COOKIES
in minutes!

FISHER
BOOKS

Publishers: Bill Fisher
                 Helen Fisher
                 Howard Fisher
Editor: Helen Fisher
Art Director: David Fischer
Cover &
Illustrations: David Fischer
Book
Production: Paula Peterson
Research
Assistant: Jan Robertson

Published by Fisher Books
P. O. Box 38040
Tucson, Arizona 85740-8040
602-292-9080

Copyright 1992 Fisher Books

Printed in U.S.A.
Printing 10 9 8 7 6 5 4 3

**Library of Congress
Cataloging-in-Publication Data**

Hoffman, Mable,
    Cookies in minutes /
  by Mable & Gar Hoffman.
        p.   cm.
    Includes index.
    ISBN 1-55561-047-1 : $9.95
    1. Cookies.   2. Quick and easy cookery.
      I. Hoffman, Gar.   II. Title.
TX772.H633   1992
641.8'654—dc20
                              92-31059
                              CIP

Notice: The information in this book is true and
complete to the best of our knowlege. It is
offered with no guarantees on the part of the
author or Fisher Books. Author and publisher
disclaim all liability in connection with use of
this book.

2

TABLE OF CONTENTS

About the Authors

A husband-and-wife team, Mable and Gar Hoffman are among the world's best-selling cookbook authors. Millions of their cookbooks are being used daily by home cooks.

The quality of their cookbooks is recognized. They've won five prestigious R. T. French Tastemaker Awards, the "Oscar" for cookbooks.

Mable and Gar own and manage Hoffman Food Consultants, Inc., which focuses on recipe development and food styling. They travel worldwide researching cuisines and innovative food ideas.

Other Fisher Books titles by Mable and Gar Hoffman are:

Crockery Favorites
Frozen Yogurt
Ice Cream, Sherbets and Sorbets
Carefree Entertaining

Acknowledgment

The Hoffmans extend a special thanks to Jan Robertson for all her invaluable assistance in recipe development and testing for **Cookies in Minutes.**

Introduction

Everybody loves cookies! They bring fond childhood memories of a busy kitchen lined with canisters of flour to be sifted and nuts to be shelled. Baking was an all-day activity.

Today we live in a world where few of us have the luxury of spending a whole day baking. We love cookies, but we don't have the time to bake them at our leisure. We need to produce great-tasting cookies in minutes.

That's why we created time-saving combinations that are sure to become favorites of your family and friends. Here are some general rules for saving minutes when making cookies.

Time-saving Tips:

- Whenever possible, buy ingredients that have some of the work already done for you. Start with nuts that are shelled and chopped, diced fruits and crushed graham crackers.

- Using one bowl for mixing saves preparation and clean-up time. Whenever possible, combine shortening and sugar in a large bowl with additional ingredients.

- Reduce time spent on actual baking by using two or three cookie sheets for drop cookies. You can fill one sheet while another one bakes. And a third one can be cooling while others are being filled or baking.

Food processors and blenders. Use them for grinding nuts, finely chopping dried fruits, pulverizing graham crackers or vanilla wafers. Note the recipes where doughs can be made in your food processor.

Electric mixers provide the fastest and most-practical way to mix most cookie doughs. If dough becomes too stiff for your mixer after all flour is added, finish stirring with a sturdy spoon.

Packaged mixes. Basic ingredients are already mixed for you in cake or pie-crust mixes and refrigerated cookies. A few additional ingredients plus the right baking procedures result in quick, tasty and easy cookies.

Refrigerated or frozen dough. Slice, add a few finishing touches and serve freshly baked cookies within minutes.

Ingredients

Shortenings
Our recipes use margarine, butter, vegetable oil, vegetable shortening or butter-flavored vegetable shortening or oil. Shortenings labeled "whipped," "diet," "light" or "spread" generally have water added and will *not* produce the same results.

Although we enjoy the flavor of butter, we suggest margarine for those who are watching their diets.

Recipes specifying vegetable shortening provide a crunchy texture. Vegetable oil, a liquid product, should not be substituted for the same amount of solid shortening. The batter will be too thin and the end result will *not* be the same.

Some recipes do call for vegetable oil. Use a mild oil, low in saturated fat. Do not use a strong-flavored oil, such as olive oil, when making cookies.

Flour
All recipes were tested with all-purpose flour or whole-wheat flour. We did not sift flour. Instead of sifting, we carefully spooned or lightly scooped flour into a dry measuring cup; then leveled off the top with a spatula or flat side of a knife.

Sugar
Our recipes call for granulated, brown, dark-brown, light-brown or powdered sugar. Molasses or honey are featured in certain recipes to make the most of their distinctive flavors. Do not substitute them for sugars unless the recipe suggests such a change.

Salt
No salt is used in these recipes. If you prefer to make cookies with salt, add it to the dough with the flour.

Eggs
For best results, use large-size, fresh eggs; all recipes using eggs were tested with them.

Flavorings
Citrus Fruits. For grated peel, grate the outside layer of fresh oranges, lemons and limes, being careful not to include the white part of the rind.

Squeeze fresh juice or use bottled juices. Lemon and orange extracts do not impart the fresh citrus flavor.

Extracts. Vanilla, almond or mint extracts will give your cookies extra flavor that makes them special. They are strong flavors, so use sparingly.

Chocolate
Semi-sweet chocolate is available in 1-ounce squares or in 6- and 12-ounce packages of tiny teardrops.

Milk chocolate or sweet chocolate is available in various size bars, as well as packages of the teardrops.

White chocolate, though not a true chocolate, is known by that name. Packages may be labeled *vanilla-milk pieces*. It is available in bars, disks and tiny teardrops.

Baking Tips

Mixing, stirring and processing
In most of our recipes ingredients are combined with an electric mixer. Whenever possible, we combined most (or all) ingredients in one large bowl, letting the mixer blend them together. At times a food processor can help you produce cookies in minutes.

Pans
Large cookie sheets with low or no sides are available in two basic sizes: 15 x 10 or 17 x 14 inches. To remove baked cookies from the pan, slide a metal spatula under them and move them to a cooling rack. Always place cookie dough on a cool baking sheet. A warm pan or sheet will result in misshapen or improperly baked cookies.

Many cooks prefer two-layered cookie sheets with air pockets. The heat distribution is more even and cookies are less likely to burn. On the other hand, bar cookies are baked in traditional baking pans.

Removing and cooling
Recipe directions tell you when to remove baked cookies. Sometimes they are easier to handle and less likely to break if cooled slightly. Place cookies in a single layer on a cooling rack. Bar cookies are cooled in the baking pan. They cool faster when pan is placed on a cooling rack.

Finishing Touches

Quick frostings & glazes
Ready-to-spread frosting. Choose from a wide variety of flavors. Just open the can, give it a quick stir; then spread on baked, cooled bar cookies. Or top each drop or refrigerator cookie with a dab of frosting; then a few chopped nuts or grated chocolate.

Citrus glaze. In small bowl, stir 1 cup powdered sugar and 2 tablespoons orange juice until smooth. Drizzle or spread over baked cooled cookies.

Lemon glaze. In small bowl, stir 3/4 cup granulated sugar with 1/4 cup lemon juice. Brush on baked cookies while they are warm.

Basic vanilla frosting. In medium bowl, combine 1/4 cup margarine or butter, 2 cups powdered sugar, 1 teaspoon vanilla and 1-1/2 to 2 tablespoons milk. Beat until smooth.

Cocoa-butter topping. In medium bowl, combine 1/3 cup margarine or butter, 1/3 cup unsweetened cocoa powder, 2 cups powdered sugar, 1 teaspoon vanilla extract and 3 tablespoons milk. Beat until smooth.

Powdered sugar

Sprinkling. Spoon 2 or 3 tablespoons powdered sugar into strainer or flour sifter. Gently shake sugar over tops of baked cookies.

Coating. Roll baked and partially cooled cookies into small bowl of powdered sugar. For a heavy coating of sugar, roll cookies in sugar a second time after they cool.

Topping. Dip one end or top of baked warm cookie in powdered sugar; hold onto sides or ends to be left plain.

Paper-doily design. Place paper doily cut-out design on top of baked and cooled cookies or pan of baked cooled bar cookies. Hold strainer with powdered sugar directly above doily. Shake sugar through strainer on to doily. Then very carefully lift and discard doily.

Colored or crystal sugar, nonpareils, chocolate shot

Balls of dough. Shape dough into 1 to 1-1/2 inch diameter balls. Roll unbaked dough in desired color; bake according to directions.

Rounds or disks. Form dough into small rounds; lightly press with a flat-bottom glass. Sprinkle tops or dip sides in decorations.

Refrigerator cookies. Before refrigerating rolls of soft dough, spread desired sugars or nonpareils on waxed paper. Roll all sides of the dough in the decorations; then wrap and refrigerate or freeze.

Sparkle with jam or jelly

Thumbprint design. Place 1-inch round of dough on cookie sheet. With thumb or forefinger, press center, forming a mini-crater. Fill with jam or jelly before baking.

Shiny coating. In microwave, heat about 2 tablespoons jelly or jam. Brush tops of sugar or spice cookies a couple of minutes after they come out of the oven.

Sandwich. Make a jam sandwich with baked and cooled peanut-butter cookies. Spread your favorite jam or jelly between two cookies; sprinkle with powdered sugar, if desired.

Chocolate designs

Chocolate drizzle. Melt one 1-ounce square semi-sweet chocolate with 1/2 teaspoon solid vegetable shortening. Then with the tip of a teaspoon, drizzle melted chocolate in a zig-zag or crisscross pattern over top of baked cooled cookies.

Layered chocolate-mint wafers. Coarsely chop mint wafers; sprinkle on hot freshly baked bar cookies.

Candy-coated chocolate pieces. Chop pieces coarsely; sprinkle on individual cookies or a pan of bars before baking.

Half-coated chocolate nuts. Dip one half of each blanched almond or cashew in melted semi-sweet or white chocolate. Or coat one half of the nuts with milk chocolate and the other half with white chocolate.

Chocolate topping. Dip tops of baked and cooled drop cookies in melted chocolate, then in finely chopped nuts.

Storing Cookies

- Thoroughly cool cookies before storing.

- Store soft cookies in container with tight-fitting lid to keep them soft.

- Store crisp cookies in container with a lid that is not tight-fitting.

- Do not store crisp cookies with soft ones.

- Waxed paper between layers keeps cookies from sticking together.

- To recrisp limp cookies, reheat a single layer on a cookie sheet in a 300F (150C) oven 4 to 6 minutes.

- Bar cookies are less likely to dry out when covered with foil or plastic wrap.

Mailing Cookies

- Choose sturdy, less-fragile types of cookies.

- Select a sturdy cardboard, plastic or metal container.

- Use plastic wrap or foil to line container, then gift wrap, if desired.

- Individually wrap very large or delicate cookies.

- Pack cookies in container between layers of bubble wrap or crumpled waxed paper.

- Bake bar cookies in foil pan, then mail in the same pan when cooled.

Drop and Bake

To many people, the drop cookie is the only *real* cookie. It is a reminder of childhood when spice-laden aromas originated in grandma's kitchen.

Drop cookies are often made of "sugar and spice and everything nice."

Unlike many other types of cookies, they appear in unusual sizes and shapes. Thick dough results in shapes resembling mini-mountain peaks. Thinner dough ends up in flat pancake-like shapes.

The size of a finished cookie depends on the amount of dough. The smaller, more delicate ones often find their way to fancy cookie trays. More hearty flavors, such as molasses and oatmeal, lend themselves to thicker and larger diameters. They usually travel well and often end up packed in lunches.

A regular teaspoon or tablespoon is easier to use than a measuring spoon when dropping dough onto a cookie sheet. To get an exact measurement, scoop a teaspoon or tablespoon of dough, then scrape across the top of spoon with table knife or small spatula to remove excess. Push dough onto cookie sheet with a smaller spoon.

When dropping dough onto cookie sheet, remember 1 rounded teaspoon of uncooked dough is about 1-1/2 teaspoons measured; 1 heaping teaspoon is about 2 teaspoons measured.

Old-Fashioned Molasses Giants

A traditional favorite, full of spices and raisins.

1/2 cup margarine or butter, room temperature
1/2 cup brown sugar, lightly packed
2 eggs
1/2 cup molasses
2 tablespoons milk
1 teaspoon baking soda
2 cups all-purpose flour
1 teaspoon ground ginger
1 teaspoon ground cinnamon
3/4 cup raisins

Preheat oven to 375F (190C). Lightly grease cookie sheets. In large bowl, beat margarine or butter, brown sugar and eggs until fluffy. Beat in molasses, milk, baking soda, flour, ginger, and cinnamon. Stir in raisins.

Drop 2 level tablespoons at a time, about 3 inches apart, on prepared cookie sheets.

Bake in preheated oven 10 to 12 minutes or until set. Remove from cookie sheets; cool on racks. Makes 21 to 23 (4-inch) cookies.

Oatmeal-Raisin Jumbos

Super-size hearty cookies made of "sugar and spice and everything nice."

2 eggs
1 cup brown sugar, lightly packed
3/4 cup vegetable oil
1 teaspoon vanilla extract
1-1/4 cups all-purpose flour
1-1/2 teaspoons baking powder
1/4 teaspoon ground allspice
1 cup quick-cooking rolled oats
3/4 cup raisins

Preheat oven to 350F (175C). In large bowl, beat eggs, sugar, vegetable oil and vanilla extract until smooth. Beat in flour, baking powder and allspice. Stir in oats and raisins.

Drop 1/4 cup at a time, about 3 inches apart, on ungreased cookie sheets.

Bake in preheated oven 14 to 16 minutes or until golden. Let stand for 1 minute. Remove from cookie sheets; cool on racks. Makes 12 jumbo (4-1/2 to 5-inch) cookies.

Peppermint-Chip Chocolate Cookies

A beautiful marriage of flavors.

1/2 cup vegetable oil
3/4 cup sugar
2 eggs
1/2 teaspoon baking soda
1-3/4 cups all-purpose flour
1/4 cup unsweetened cocoa powder
2/3 cup crushed peppermint candies (about 22 small rounds)

Preheat oven to 375F (190C). Grease cookie sheets. In large bowl, beat oil, sugar, eggs, soda, flour and cocoa until smooth. Reserve about 3 tablespoons crushed peppermint for tops of cookies; add remaining to dough.

Drop dough by rounded teaspoons, about 2 inches apart, on prepared cookie sheets.

Bake in preheated oven 8 to 10 minutes or until firm. Immediately remove to cooling rack and sprinkle each hot cookie with reserved crushed candies. If difficult to remove from cookie sheets, return to oven 2 to 3 minutes to soften. Makes 45 to 50.

Tip
To crush peppermint, place small, round, hard, red-and-white candies in plastic bag. Gently pound them into chips or small chunks with a wooden mallet.

Pine-Nut Crispies

As soon as these cookies cool they become very crunchy.

1 cup brown sugar, lightly packed
2 eggs
2 tablespoons melted margarine or butter
1 teaspoon vanilla extract
3/4 cup all-purpose flour
3/4 cup toasted pine nuts

Preheat oven to 350F (175C). Grease *and* flour cookie sheets. In medium bowl, beat together brown sugar, eggs, margarine, vanilla extract and flour. Stir in pine nuts.

Drop by teaspoon, about 2 inches apart, on prepared cookie sheets.

Bake in preheated oven 7 to 9 minutes or until golden around the edges. Remove from cookie sheets; cool on racks. Makes about 34.

Tip
If these soften, recrisp them in a 350F (175C) oven
4 or 5 minutes.

Peanut-Lovers' Cookies

Enjoy peanut-butter flavor with the crunchiness of chopped peanuts.

1/2 cup peanut butter
1/2 cup vegetable shortening
3/4 cup brown sugar, lightly packed
1 egg
1 cup all-purpose flour
1 teaspoon baking powder
1/2 cup chopped peanuts
2 to 3 tablespoons peanut halves

Preheat oven to 350F (175C). In large bowl, beat peanut butter, shortening, brown sugar and egg until well blended. Stir in flour, baking powder and chopped peanuts.

Drop by rounded teaspoon, about 2 inches apart, on ungreased cookie sheets. Flatten slightly. Place 1/2 of a peanut in center of each.

Bake in preheated oven 8 to 10 minutes or until golden brown. Remove from cookie sheets; cool on racks. Makes 40 to 45.

Tip
To flatten unbaked cookies, dip the base of a flat-bottom glass into granulated sugar; then lightly press on top of each unbaked cookie after it is on the baking pan.

Piña-Colada Date Mounds

If piña-colada yogurt is not available, substitute apricot-pineapple, orange, or other tropical flavors.

1/2 cup margarine or butter, room temperature
3/4 cup sugar
2 egg whites
6 oz. piña-colada lowfat yogurt
1 teaspoon baking powder
1/2 teaspoon baking soda
1-1/2 cups all-purpose flour
3/4 cup chopped dates
1 cup uncooked old-fashioned rolled oats
Powdered sugar

Preheat oven to 375F (190C). In large bowl, beat margarine, sugar, egg whites, yogurt, baking powder, soda and flour. Stir in dates and oats.

Drop by rounded tablespoon of dough, about 2 inches apart, on ungreased cookie sheets.

Bake in preheated oven 13 to 15 minutes. Sift powdered sugar over tops of warm cookies. Remove from cookie sheets; cool on racks. Makes 25 to 30.

Mincemeat Oatmeal Drops

Mincemeat adds flavor and spicy accents to this quick-and-easy cookie.

1 egg, beaten slightly
3/4 cup brown sugar, lightly packed
1/2 cup vegetable oil
3/4 teaspoon baking soda
1-1/4 cups all-purpose flour
1 cup prepared mincemeat
1-1/4 cups quick-cooking rolled oats

Preheat oven to 350F (175C). Grease cookie sheets. In large bowl, combine egg, sugar, oil, soda, flour, mincemeat and oats.

Drop by teaspoon, about 2 inches apart, on prepared cookie sheets.

Bake in preheated oven 9 to 11 minutes or until golden brown. Remove from cookie sheets; cool on racks. Makes 40 to 45.

South Pacific Dreams

Surprise your guests with island flavors of coconut and ginger.

1/3 cup brown sugar, lightly packed
1/3 cup vegetable oil
1 egg
1/2 teaspoon almond extract
3/4 cup all-purpose flour
1/4 cup flaked coconut
2 tablespoons finely chopped candied ginger
1 to 1-1/2 tablespoons toasted sesame seeds

Preheat oven to 350F (175C). In medium bowl, beat brown sugar, vegetable oil, egg, almond extract and flour. Stir in coconut and ginger.

Drop by rounded teaspoons, about 2 inches apart, on ungreased cookie sheets. Sprinkle with sesame seeds.

Bake in preheated oven 9 to 11 minutes or until golden. Remove from cookie sheets; cool on racks. Makes 20 to 22.

Tip
Let the sesame seeds toast in a pie pan in 350F (175C) oven while you're mixing the cookie dough.

Double-Chocolate Bittersweet Surprise

A not-so-sweet rich cookie flavored with cocoa and large chocolate pieces.

1/2 cup butter-flavored vegetable shortening
3/4 cup sugar
1/4 cup unsweetened cocoa powder
1 egg
1 teaspoon vanilla extract
1-1/4 cups all-purpose flour
1/4 teaspoon baking soda
1 cup semi-sweet chocolate chunks or large chips (6 oz.)

Preheat oven to 350F (175C). In large bowl, beat shortening, sugar, cocoa, egg and vanilla extract until well blended. Stir in flour and soda; then chocolate chunks.

Drop one level tablespoon at a time, about 2 inches apart, on ungreased cookie sheets.

Bake in preheated oven 11 to 14 minutes or until firm. Remove from cookie sheets; cool on racks. Makes 33 to 35.

Chocolate Butterfinger® Mounds

Crunchy meringue-like cookies disappear as soon as they are served.

2 egg whites, room temperature
1/2 cup powdered sugar
1 cup finely crushed chocolate-cookie crumbs (about 12 cookies)
1 (2.1-oz.) Butterfinger® candy bar, coarsely chopped

Preheat oven to 325F (165C). Grease cookie sheets. In medium bowl, beat egg whites until soft peaks form. Gradually add powdered sugar; beat until very stiff. Fold in chocolate-cookie crumbs and chopped candy bar.

Drop by teaspoon, about 2 inches apart, on prepared cookie sheets.

Bake in preheated oven 17 to 20 minutes. Remove from cookie sheets; cool on racks. Makes 21 to 23.

Golden Granola Rounds

Not too sweet, filled with nutritious raisins, carrots and sunflower seeds.

1/3 cup margarine or butter, room temperature
1/3 cup brown sugar, lightly packed
1/2 teaspoon ground cinnamon
1 egg
3/4 cup granola
3/4 cup all-purpose flour
1/4 teaspoon baking soda
1 large carrot, finely grated (about 1 cup)
1/2 cup hulled sunflower seeds
1/2 cup raisins

Preheat oven to 375F (190C). Lightly grease cookie sheets. In large bowl, beat margarine, brown sugar, cinnamon and egg. Beat in granola, flour and soda. Stir in carrot, sunflower seeds and raisins.

Drop by rounded tablespoon, about 2 inches apart, on prepared cookie sheet. With back of spoon, flatten to about 1/4 inch thickness.

Bake in preheated oven 8 to 9 minutes or until light brown. Remove from cookie sheet; cool on racks. Makes about 18.

Pronto Date-Sesame Drops

Rich flavors combine to make this extra-special treat.

1/3 cup toasted sesame seeds
3 tablespoons all-purpose flour
1/2 cup brown sugar, lightly packed
1 egg, beaten slightly
1/2 teaspoon vanilla extract
1 tablespoon margarine or butter, melted
1 tablespoon finely chopped crystallized ginger
1/4 cup finely chopped dates

Preheat oven to 350F (175C). Grease *and* flour baking sheets. In medium bowl, combine toasted sesame seeds, flour and sugar. Add egg, vanilla extract, margarine, crystallized ginger and dates; stir until well blended.

Drop about 1 tablespoon mixture on prepared baking sheets. With back of spoon, spread to about 2-1/2 inches in diameter.

Bake in preheated oven 6 to 7 minutes or until edges begin to brown. Remove from cookie sheet; cool on racks. Makes about 15 (3-inch) cookies.

Tip
Toast sesame seeds in shallow baking pan in preheated oven 5 to 7 minutes, stirring once or twice. To save time, toast a double batch of 2/3 cup and save half for the next time.

Mix 'n Drop Sugar Rounds

Decorate as faces or with a drizzle of frosting.

2 eggs, beaten slightly
3/4 cup sugar
3/4 cup vegetable oil
1-1/2 teaspoons vanilla extract
1 teaspoon baking powder
2 cups all-purpose flour
Vegetable oil and sugar for topping

Preheat oven to 375F (190C). In large bowl, stir together eggs, 3/4 cup sugar, 3/4 cup vegetable oil and vanilla extract. Add baking powder and flour.

Drop by heaping tablespoon, about 2 inches apart, on ungreased cookie sheets. Lightly press each cookie to about 3 inches in diameter with bottom of a flat-bottom glass that has been brushed with oil, then dipped in sugar.

Bake in preheated oven 10 to 12 minutes. Remove from cookie sheets; cool on racks. Decorate, as desired. Makes 16 to 18.

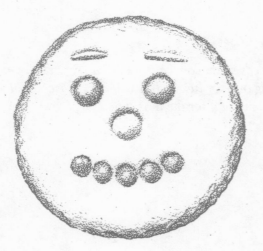

Banana Chocolate-Chip Snackers

A favorite lunchbox or after-school treat.

2 ripe medium bananas, peeled and quartered
1/2 cup light-brown sugar, lightly packed
1/4 cup molasses
1 egg
1/3 cup margarine or butter, room temperature
1/2 cup nonfat dry-milk powder
1-1/4 cups all-purpose flour
1/4 cup oat bran
1 teaspoon baking powder
1/2 teaspoon baking soda
1/8 teaspoon ground ginger
1-1/2 cups semi-sweet chocolate pieces or chunks (9 or 10 oz.)

Preheat oven to 350F (175C). In large bowl, beat bananas and brown sugar until almost smooth. Beat in molasses, egg, margarine, dry-milk powder, flour, oat bran, baking powder, baking soda and ginger. Stir in chocolate pieces or chunks.

Drop by heaping teaspoons, about 2 inches apart, on ungreased cookie sheets.

Bake in preheated oven about 10 minutes or until cookies begin to brown. Remove from cookie sheets; cool on racks. Makes about 48 cookies.

Traditional Chocolate-Chip Cookies

Without a doubt, the all-time favorite.

1 cup margarine or butter, room temperature
3/4 cup granulated sugar
3/4 cup brown sugar, firmly packed
1 teaspoon vanilla extract
2 eggs
2-1/4 cups all-purpose flour
1 teaspoon baking soda
1(12-oz.) package semi-sweet chocolate pieces (2 cups)
1 cup coarsely chopped walnuts

Preheat oven to 375F (190C). In large bowl, beat margarine, granulated and brown sugar, vanilla extract and eggs until creamy. Beat in flour and baking soda. Stir in chocolate pieces and nuts.

Drop by heaping teaspoons on ungreased cookie sheets.

Bake in preheated oven 8 to 10 minutes. Remove from cookie sheets; cool on racks. Makes about 60 to 65.

Tip
The original recipe calls for 1 teaspoon salt. We tested without this ingredient, but if you like it with salt add 1 teaspoon with the flour.

No-Bake Treasures

Technically, these unbaked treats are *not* cookies. They fall into a category between a candy and a cookie. It doesn't really matter what you call them. After you try several, you'll realize that they're wonderful treats for family get-togethers. Most of them are good travelers; ideal for transporting anywhere from the local park to servicemen in far-off lands.

Most of them are quick and easy to put together. Parents encourage children to start their cookie-making with no-bakes; then let them graduate to more complicated specialties requiring the use of an oven.

If you prefer, use your microwave oven for melting and combining ingredients rather than a saucepan on the stove top.

On a steamy summer day, it's a real treat to enjoy a fresh cookie and a frosty glass of lemonade or iced tea without the discomfort of additional oven heat.

Cold cereals, nuts, dried fruits and crushed candies are favorite ingredients in these no-bakes. Remember that many of these recipes are finger foods and must be refrigerated for an hour or more to solidify ingredients before cutting or picking up.

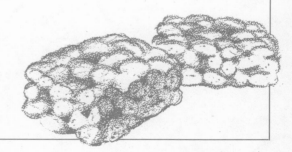

Macadamia White-Chocolate Bars

Lots of tasty bits and pieces combined in a bar that doesn't require baking.

1 (12-oz.) package vanilla-milk or white-chocolate pieces (2 cups)
1/4 cup milk
1/4 cup margarine or butter
1/2 teaspoon vanilla extract
3 cups O-shaped oat cereal
1/2 cup chopped macadamia nuts
3/4 cup flaked coconut

Grease bottom and sides of an 8-inch-square pan. In large saucepan, combine vanilla-milk pieces, milk and margarine over low heat until melted. Remove from heat. Add vanilla extract, cereal, macadamia nuts and coconut.

Press evenly in prepared pan. Refrigerate 1 hour or until firm. Cut into bars. Makes 20 to 25.

Tip:
*Use your microwave to melt vanilla-milk pieces, milk
and margarine.*

Red-Hot Apple Cereal Clusters

Children love these bright-pink treats.

2 tablespoons margarine or butter
2 cups miniature marshmallows (or 20 large)
1/2 cup cinnamon red-hot candies
3 cups puffed rice
1/2 cup finely chopped dried apples

Grease an 8-inch-square pan. In large saucepan, melt margarine, marshmallows and red-hots over low heat, stirring often until candy is almost completely melted. Add remaining ingredients, mixing well.

Press firmly in prepared pan. Chill until set. Cut or pull off clusters. Makes about 20 servings.

Fig Crunchies

Make them at a moment's notice in your food processor.

2 cups corn- or wheat-flake cereal
3/4 cup dried figs, quartered (7 or 8)
1/3 cup pecans or walnuts
1 tablespoon orange juice
1/2 teaspoon grated orange peel
2 tablespoons margarine or butter, melted
2 tablespoons corn syrup
3 to 4 tablespoons powdered sugar

In food processor, combine all ingredients except powdered sugar. Process until finely chopped.

Shape into 1-inch balls; roll in powdered sugar. Makes 18 to 20.

No-Bake Chocolate-Marshmallow Peaks

Savor these creamy chocolate morsels.

1/4 cup margarine or butter
3 cups miniature marshmallows
1 cup semi-sweet chocolate pieces
1 cup powdered sugar
1 teaspoon vanilla extract
3/4 cup flaked coconut
1/2 cup chopped pecans

In a large saucepan, combine margarine and marshmallows; heat over low temperature until melted. Remove from heat. Stir in chocolate pieces until melted; then add powdered sugar, vanilla extract, coconut and pecans.

Drop by teaspoons on wax-paper-lined tray or cookie sheet. Refrigerate at least 1/2 hour or until firm. Makes 30-32.

Tip
By mixing all ingredients in one pan you save extra clean-up and dishwashing.

Chocolate Irish-Cream Balls

Reward yourself with this sinfully divine cookie.

2-1/2 cups finely crushed chocolate cookies (38 to 40)
3/4 cup powdered sugar
1/2 cup finely chopped walnuts
2 tablespoons corn syrup
1/3 cup Irish-Cream liqueur
3 tablespoons powdered sugar for coating

In large bowl, combine crushed cookies, 3/4 cup powdered sugar, nuts, corn syrup and Irish Cream.

Pinch off small amount of dough; with hands, roll into 1-inch balls. Roll in additional powdered sugar. Lightly tap to shake off excess sugar. Makes 32 to 34.

Tip
Use the entire 9-oz. box of thin dark-chocolate cookies for this delicious recipe.

Chocolate Date Snackers

A great quick-to-fix accompaniment to a cup of tea.

26 graham-cracker squares
1 (15.5-oz.) can ready-to-spread chocolate coconut-almond frosting
2 tablespoons margarine or butter, melted
1/2 cup chopped dates
1/4 cup powdered sugar for coating

Coarsely crumble graham crackers with rolling pin or hands. In large bowl, combine crushed graham crackers, frosting, margarine and dates.

Form into 1-inch balls. Roll in powdered sugar. Makes about 48.

Chocolate Almond-Cherry Bites

Festive red and green candied cherries in holiday dress with cookie crumbs.

2 cups powdered sugar
2 tablespoons unsweetened cocoa powder
1/2 cup margarine or butter, melted
1/2 teaspoon almond extract
1/4 cup finely chopped slivered toasted almonds
20-25 candied red or green cherries
6 chocolate cookies, crushed (about 1/2 cup)

In medium bowl, beat sugar, cocoa, margarine, almond extract and almonds until well blended.

Form 1 tablespoon mixture around each cherry; then roll in cookie crumbs. Makes 20-25.

Decadent Temptations

Impossible to resist.

1 cup milk-chocolate pieces (6 oz.)
1/4 cup margarine or butter
2 teaspoons vegetable oil
12 crisp chocolate-chip cookies, coarsely chopped (about 2 cups)
3/4 cup powdered sugar
1/2 cup peanut butter
2 tablespoons margarine or butter, room temperature

Line a 9-inch-square pan with foil. In medium saucepan over very low heat, combine chocolate pieces, 1/4 cup margarine and oil. Stir until melted. Add cookie pieces and mix well.

Press firmly in bottom of prepared pan. In medium bowl, stir together powdered sugar, peanut butter and 2 tablespoons margarine until well blended.

Spread over cookie mixture in pan. Chill at least 1 hour. Lift foil and temptations out of pan. Cut into small pieces. Makes 30 to 34.

No-Bake Pastel Haystacks

Delicate colors add a festive touch to your tray of cookies.

1 cup vanilla-milk or white-chocolate pieces
1 tablespoon finely chopped candied ginger
1/2 cup coarsely chopped cashew nuts
1 cup chow-mein noodles
1/2 cup pastel-colored miniature marshmallows

In medium saucepan, melt vanilla-milk pieces over very low heat. Remove from heat. Stir in ginger, cashews, noodles and marshmallows.

Drop by teaspoon on wax paper; chill. Makes about 20 to 22.

> **Tip**
> *Most of us know vanilla-milk pieces as white-chocolate pieces, but they cannot legally be labeled as such when made and sold in the United States.*

Skillet Fruit Bars

At their crispy best the day they're made.

1/2 cup margarine or butter
1/2 cup brown sugar, lightly packed
1 egg, beaten slightly
1/2 cup mixed dried fruits, chopped
1/2 cup flaked coconut
2 cups crisp rice cereal
1 teaspoon vanilla extract

Lightly grease a 9-inch-square baking pan. Melt margarine in 10-inch skillet. Remove from heat. Add sugar and egg. Return to heat; cook and stir over low heat until mixture simmers. Remove from heat; stir in dried fruits, coconut, cereal and vanilla extract.

Cool slightly; firmly press into prepared pan. Cool; cut into small bars. Makes 35 to 40.

Rocky Road Samples

Each bite will have you reaching for one more.

1/4 cup sugar
1/4 cup light corn syrup
1/3 cup margarine or butter
1/2 cup miniature marshmallows
1/4 cup unsweetened cocoa powder
1 teaspoon vanilla extract
2 cups muesli

In medium saucepan, over low heat, combine sugar, corn syrup, margarine, marshmallows and cocoa; stir until marshmallows melt. Remove from heat. Add vanilla extract and muesli.

Place about 35 small crinkled-paper cups on a small tray. Spoon about 1 tablespoon mixture into each cup. Refrigerate on tray about 30 minutes until firm. Makes about 35.

Tip
Small crinkled cups are the kind used to hold individual pieces of chocolate candy. Sold at stores selling cake-decorating supplies.

Speedy Chocolate Peanut-Butter Balls

A super-quickie cookie. Best when served after chilling.

1/4 cup peanut butter
1/4 cup chocolate syrup
2/3 cup graham-cracker crumbs
1/3 cup coarsely chopped peanuts

In medium bowl, combine peanut butter and syrup. Stir in crumbs. Form into 1-inch balls. Roll each ball in chopped peanuts; chill, if desired. Makes 16 to 18.

Tip
Lightly spread the palms of your hands with butter or margarine before forming balls.

Make Your Own Cookie Mixes

Your own cookie mixes are time-saving and handy to have ready for unexpected guests. We designed five mixes you can use for an unbelievable variety of cookies. All of our mixes contain basic ingredients; then suggestions for additions to make different varieties.

Each mix makes two batches of cookies when ingredients from variations are added. Using a food processor or mixer to mix the basic ingredients produces greater volume than the separate quantities might indicate. We included two different recipes for each mix.

Obviously, a heavy-duty mixer or large food processor is ideal. While it may take longer, it can be done with standard equipment. If the mixture is too heavy for your mixer or processor, mix half the amount; then repeat mixing the other half.

Store the dry mix in an airtight container in a cool, dry place. Use it within two months. We divide each double batch into 2 equal parts and store each in separate plastic bags. Keep them in an airtight container until needed. Label each with the mix name and date it was prepared.

All-Purpose Cookie Mix

Use one-half for a batch of Cookie Pops, the other half for Orange Cranberry Nut Surprise.

4 cups all-purpose flour
2 teaspoons baking powder
1-1/2 cups vegetable shortening
1 cup instant nonfat dry-milk powder
2 cups granulated sugar

In food processor or electric mixer at low speed, combine flour, baking powder, shortening, nonfat dry-milk powder and sugar. Process until mixture is texture of fine crumbs.

Store in covered plastic or glass container in cool dry place. Makes 10 cups mix or 2 batches of Cookie Pops or Orange Cranberry Nut Surprise. (See pages 42 and 43).

Cookie Pops

Just the right surprise treat for kids at a birthday or holiday celebration.

1 batch (5 cups) Basic All-Purpose Cookie Mix
1 egg, beaten slightly
1/2 teaspoon vanilla extract
1/4 cup water
Coarsely crushed hard candies, red-hots, raisins and nonpareils

Preheat oven to 375F (190C). In large bowl, stir 1 batch or 5 cups Basic All-Purpose Cookie Mix, egg, vanilla extract and water until well blended. Form into 1-1/2-inch balls.

Place 3 inches apart on ungreased cookie sheets. Insert popsicle stick halfway into each cookie. With flat-bottom glass dipped in sugar, press top of cookie to about 2-1/2 inch diameter. Sprinkle with your choice of candies.

Bake in preheated oven about 15 minutes or until edges are slightly browned. Remove from cookie sheets; cool on racks. Makes about 18 (4-inch) pops.

Orange-Cranberry Nut Surprise

Great flavor combination of bright-red cranberry pieces peeking through the orange-flavored topping.

1 batch (5 cups) All-Purpose Cookie Mix
1 egg, beaten slightly
1/3 cup orange juice
1/2 teaspoon grated orange peel
1 cup cranberries, coarsely chopped
1/2 cup chopped walnuts
Citrus Glaze, page 7

Preheat oven to 350F (175C). In large bowl, combine 1 batch or 5 cups All-Purpose Cookie Mix, egg, orange juice, peel, cranberries and walnuts.

Drop by teaspoons, about 2 inches apart, on ungreased cookie sheets .

Bake in preheated oven 10 to 15 minutes or until set. Remove from cookie sheets; cool on racks 5 to 10 minutes. Dip tops of cooled cookies into Citrus Glaze. Makes 48 to 52.

Bar-Cookie Mix

Use one-half this mix for a batch of Date and Nut Bars, the other half for Praline Cream Bars.

4 cups all-purpose flour
1 cup granulated sugar
2 teaspoons baking powder
1 cup vegetable shortening

In food processor or electric mixer at low speed, combine flour, sugar, baking powder and shortening. Process until mixture resembles coarse cornmeal.

Store in covered glass or plastic container in cool dry place. Makes 7 cups mix or 2 batches Date and Nut Bars or Praline Cream Bars. See pages 45 and 46.

Date and Nut Bars

Maple syrup and dates make these irresistible.

1 batch (3-1/2 cups) Bar Cookie Mix
1/3 cup maple syrup
2 eggs, beaten slightly
1/2 teaspoon baking soda
1/4 cup milk
1 cup chopped pitted dates
1/2 cup chopped walnuts
Citrus Glaze, page 7

Preheat oven to 350F (175C). Grease 13 x 9-inch baking pan. In large bowl, combine 1 batch (3-1/2 cups) Bar Cookie Mix, maple syrup, eggs, baking soda, milk, dates and nuts. Spread into prepared pan.

Bake in preheated oven 20 to 25 minutes or until wooden toothpick inserted in center comes out clean.

Cool in pan. Drizzle with Citrus Glaze. Cut into bars. Makes 30 to 40.

Tip
If you are short of time, buy dates and nuts that are already chopped.

Praline Cream Bars

Your taste buds will transport you to New Orleans.

1 batch (3-1/2 cups) Bar-Cookie Mix
1/4 cup chopped pecans
1 egg, beaten slightly

Topping:
1/3 cup brown sugar, lightly packed
1 (3-oz.) pkg. cream cheese, room temperature
1/2 teaspoon vanilla extract
1 egg
3/4 cup butterscotch pieces

Preheat oven to 350F (175C). In large bowl, combine 1 batch or 3-1/2 cups Bar-Cookie Mix, pecans and one egg. Pat on bottom of ungreased 9-inch-square baking pan. Bake in preheated oven 15 to 20 minutes.

Topping:
Beat sugar and cream cheese. Add vanilla extract and one egg, beating until smooth; stir in butterscotch pieces. Spoon over partially baked cookie crust. Return pan to oven.

Bake an additional 15 to 20 minutes or until firm on top. Cool in pan; cut into bars or squares. Store in refrigerator. Makes 24 to 32.

> **Tip**
> *Always refrigerate baked bars that contain dairy products.*

Chocolate-Cookie Mix

Chocolate-Cookie Mix makes 1 recipe of Chocolate Jewels plus 1 recipe of Chocolate Sprinkle Rounds.

5 cups all-purpose flour
2 teaspoons baking soda
2/3 cup unsweetened cocoa powder
3 cups granulated sugar

Combine flour, baking soda, cocoa and sugar. Store in covered plastic or glass container in cool dry place. Makes 8 cups mix or 2 batches of Chocolate Jewels or Chocolate Sprinkle Rounds.

Chocolate Jewels

A chocolate-drop cookie studded with jewel-like colorful candies.

1-1/2 cups candy-coated chocolate pieces (12 oz.)
1 batch (4 cups) Chocolate-Cookie Mix
2 eggs, beaten slightly
1/2 cup vegetable oil
1/3 cup milk
1 teaspoon vanilla extract

Remove 1/4 cup candies, coarsely chop; set aside. Preheat oven to 350F (175C). Lightly grease cookie sheets. In large bowl, combine one batch Chocolate-Cookie Mix, eggs, vegetable oil, milk, vanilla extract and whole candy-coated chocolate pieces.

Drop rounded teaspoons 2 inches apart on prepared cookie sheets. Sprinkle with chopped candies.

Bake in preheated oven 12 to 14 minutes or until firm. Remove from cookie sheets; cool on racks. Makes about 48.

Chocolate Sprinkle Rounds

Chocolate sprinkles add just the right finishing touch.

1 batch (4 cups) Chocolate-Cookie Mix
2 eggs
3/4 cup butter-flavored vegetable shortening
1 teaspoon vanilla extract
2 tablespoons milk
1/3 cup chocolate sprinkles

Preheat oven to 350F (175C). In large bowl, beat Chocolate-Cookie Mix, eggs, butter-flavored shortening, vanilla extract and milk.

Form into 1-inch balls. Dip tops in chocolate sprinkles. Place 2 inches apart on ungreased cookie sheets.

Bake in preheated oven 10 to 12 minutes or until firm. Remove from cookie sheets; cool on racks. Makes about 65.

Oatmeal-Cookie Mix

This basic mix makes 2 batches of Hasty Oatmeal Fruit Drops or Spiced-Apple Oatmeal Bars.

2 cups all-purpose flour
1 teaspoon baking soda
2 cups brown sugar, lightly packed
2/3 cup granulated sugar
1-1/2 cups vegetable shortening
6 cups quick-cooking rolled oats

With mixer at low speed, mix all ingredients. Store in covered plastic or glass container in cool dry place. Makes about 12-1/2 cups of mix or 2 batches of Spiced-Apple Oatmeal Bars or Hasty Oatmeal Fruit Drops (pages 51 and 52).

Spiced-Apple Oatmeal Bars

Thoroughly cool bars in the pan before cutting into desired shapes.

1 batch (6-1/4 cups) Oatmeal-Cookie Mix
2 eggs
1 cup applesauce
1/2 cup orange juice
1/2 teaspoon ground cinnamon
1/2 teaspoon ground ginger
1/2 teaspoon baking powder
3/4 cup raisins

Spice Glaze:
1 cup powdered sugar
1/8 teaspoon ground nutmeg
2 tablespoons milk

Preheat oven to 350F (175C). Grease a 13 x 9-inch baking pan. In large bowl, beat 1 batch Oatmeal-Cookie Mix (6-1/4 cups), eggs, applesauce, orange juice, spices and baking powder until well blended. Stir in raisins. Spread in prepared pan.

Bake in preheated oven 25 to 30 minutes or until toothpick comes out clean when inserted in center. Cool in pan. Top with glaze, if desired. Cut in bars or squares. Makes 24 to 32.

Spice Glaze:
In a small bowl, combine ingredients; spread over cool bars.

Hasty Oatmeal Fruit Drops

Slightly chewy cookie with flavor accents of a variety of fruits.

1/2 cup milk
1 egg, beaten slightly
1 teaspoon vanilla extract
1 batch (6-1/4 cups) Oatmeal-Cookie Mix
1 cup dried-fruit bits

Preheat oven to 350F (175C). In large bowl, beat milk, egg, vanilla extract and 1 batch Oatmeal-Cookie Mix (6-1/4 cups). Stir in fruit bits.

Drop by heaping teaspoons, about 2 inches apart, on ungreased cookie sheets.

Bake in preheated oven 12 to 15 minutes or until golden brown. Remove from cookie sheets; cool on racks. Makes about 50.

Brownie Mix

This basic brownie mix makes two batches of Kissing Temptations or Butterscotch Chocolate Chews.

2 cups granulated sugar
2/3 cup unsweetened cocoa powder
1 teaspoon baking powder
1-1/2 cups all-purpose flour

In large bowl, combine sugar, cocoa, baking powder and flour. Store in covered plastic or glass container in cool dry place. Makes 4 cups or 2 batches of Kissing Temptations or Butterscotch Chocolate Chews (pages 54 and 55).

Kissing Temptations

Surprise! There's a candy kiss in the middle.

1 batch (2 cups) Brownie Mix
1/3 cup margarine or butter, room temperature
1 egg
1 teaspoon vanilla extract
30 to 34 milk-chocolate candy kisses, unwrapped

Preheat oven to 350F (175C). In large bowl, beat 1 batch Brownie Mix (2 cups), margarine, egg and vanilla extract until well blended.

Wrap a heaping teaspoon of dough around each kiss. Place 2 inches apart on ungreased cookie sheets.

Bake in preheated oven 8 to 10 minutes or until set. Remove from cookie sheets; cool on racks. Makes 30 to 34.

Butterscotch Chocolate Chews

Butterscotch pieces provide an interesting substitute for frosting on this brownie-like bar.

1 batch (2 cups) Brownie Mix
1/2 cup melted margarine or butter
2 eggs, beaten slightly
1 teaspoon vanilla extract
3/4 cup butterscotch pieces

Preheat oven to 350F (175C). Grease a 9-inch-square baking pan. In large bowl, combine 2 cups Brownie Mix, margarine, eggs and vanilla extract until well blended. Pour into prepared pan.

Bake in preheated oven about 25 minutes or until edges begin to leave sides of pan. Remove from oven. Immediately sprinkle top with butterscotch pieces; then return to oven 2 to 3 minutes. Cool in pan; cut into bars. Makes 24 to 32.

Stir and Microwave

Yes, you can produce good-tasting cookies in your microwave. And they are ready in minutes!

After much experimenting, we agree that all cookies should not be microwaved. In most cases, it is more practical to bake a large batch of cookies in a traditional oven. With limited space in a microwave, it takes too long to bake 50 or 60 cookies. However, we've developed a number of successful microwave treats.

When using the microwave, we found several handy baking dishes. The 8-inch-square microwavable dish was the most practical for recipes like Peanut-Butter Milk-Chocolate Favorites and Mississippi-Mud Bars. To make a few individual cookies, we prefer a microwavable pizza plate or traditional pie plate.

To microwave evenly, we rotated the baking dish one quarter turn every minute during the cooking process. Due to the speed of microwaving, we checked the cookies on every turn; then removed the dish when the cookie tops were slightly dry to the touch.

Fudgy Mint Squares

Serve these rich chocolate-mint bars with vanilla ice cream.

1/2 cup semi-sweet chocolate pieces (3 oz.)
3/4 cup margarine or butter
1 cup brown sugar, lightly packed
1 teaspoon vanilla extract
1/4 teaspoon baking powder
1 egg, beaten slightly
1 cup all-purpose flour
1 cup mint-flavored chocolate pieces (6 oz.)

Grease an 8-inch-square microwavable baking dish. In 1-quart glass measure or microwavable bowl, combine semi-sweet chocolate and margarine.

Microwave on high 1 minute. Stir; microwave an additional 30 seconds or until almost melted. Stir until smooth. Mix in sugar, vanilla extract, baking powder, egg and flour. Fold in mint-chocolate pieces. Pour into prepared dish.

Microwave on high about 4-1/2 minutes or until center is bubbly, turning dish a quarter turn after each minute. Cool in pan. Refrigerate at least 1 hour; cut into squares. Makes 20 to 25.

Tip
If there are no semi-sweet chocolate pieces in your cupboard, substitute three squares of semi-sweet chocolate. Coarsely chop them for ease in melting with margarine.

Granola Peanut-Butter Chunks

A snack that's easy to make—great to sample.

2 cups granola
1/2 cup plain candy-coated chocolate pieces, coarsely chopped
1/4 cup peanut butter
1/4 cup honey
1 egg, beaten slightly
1/3 cup raisins

Grease an 8-inch-square microwavable dish. In medium bowl, combine ingredients. Press into bottom of prepared dish.

Microwave on high 3-1/2 minutes, turning dish a quarter turn once every minute.

Partially cool in baking dish at room temperature; then refrigerate. Cut into chunks or break off small pieces. Makes about 25 pieces.

Hurry-Up Shortbread Strips

A delicious variation of Scottish shortbread features toasted almonds.

1/2 cup toasted blanched almonds
1/2 cup margarine or butter
1/4 cup brown sugar, lightly packed
1/8 teaspoon almond extract
1 cup all-purpose flour
Powdered sugar

In food processor, grind almonds. Add remaining ingredients. Mix just until it clings together in a ball. Divide dough in half. In 11 x 7-inch rectangular microwavable baking dish, pat one half of dough about 10-1/2 by 2-1/2 inches down one side of dish. Pat remaining dough down other side, being careful to leave a 1-1/2 inch space down middle of dish between dough strips.

Microwave on high 4 to 4-1/2 minutes, turning dish a quarter turn every minute.

While warm, cut into bars about 3-1/4 by 1 inch. When cool, sift powdered sugar over top. Makes 20 to 22.

Tip
To save time, process almonds first; then add remaining ingredients to processor.

Top-Hat Cookies

Dress up a plain sugar cookie.

3 tablespoons thick hot-fudge ice-cream topping
8 store-bought or homemade sugar cookies, about 2-1/2 to 3 inches
4 large marshmallows, halved crosswise
2 tablespoons chopped peanuts

In small microwavable bowl, heat fudge sauce on high 30 to 45 seconds; set aside. Place cookies on 12-inch-round microwavable dish.

Top each with a marshmallow half; heat on high 15 to 20 seconds or until marshmallows puff.

Top each with about 1 teaspoon of heated fudge sauce. Sprinkle with peanuts. Makes 8.

Tip
If you don't have a 12-inch microwavable dish, heat 4 cookies at a time in a 9-inch pie plate 10 to 15 seconds. Repeat with remaining cookies.

Toffee Chocolate Bars

So good they seem to melt in your mouth.

Crust:
3/4 cup brown sugar, lightly packed
1/3 cup margarine or butter, room temperature
1-1/2 cups all-purpose flour
1/2 cup chopped walnuts or pecans

Topping:
1/2 cup margarine or butter
1/2 cup brown sugar, lightly packed
1 cup semi-sweet chocolate pieces (6 oz.)

Crust:
In medium bowl, beat 3/4 cup brown sugar, 1/3 cup margarine and flour until well mixed and crumbly. Press in bottom of an 8-inch-square microwavable baking dish. Top with nuts. Microwave on high 2-1/2 minutes, turning dish a quarter turn after every minute. Remove from microwave; set aside.

Topping:
In 2-cup microwavable measure, combine 1/2 cup margarine and 1/2 cup brown sugar; microwave on high 1-3/4 to 2 minutes or until margarine melts and mixture is bubbly. Pour over partially baked crust. Microwave on high 2 minutes, turning dish a quarter turn after first minute. Immediately sprinkle with chocolate pieces. Cool in pan at room temperature. Then refrigerate for 1 hour. Cut into bars. Makes 20 to 25.

Tip
It is not absolutely necessary to refrigerate baked cookies. Chilling solidifies the chocolate pieces, making them easier to handle.

Peanut-Butter Milk-Chocolate Favorites

For variety, substitute plain or multi-colored candy-coated semi-sweet chocolate pieces for the milk chocolate.

2/3 cup brown sugar, lightly packed
1/3 cup crunchy peanut butter
2 tablespoons margarine or butter
1 egg
1/2 teaspoon vanilla extract
1/2 teaspoon baking powder
1/2 cup all-purpose flour
1/2 cup milk-chocolate pieces
Powdered sugar, if desired

Very lightly grease a microwavable 8-inch-square baking dish. In medium bowl, beat sugar, peanut butter, margarine, egg and vanilla extract until fluffy. Beat in baking powder and flour. Stir in chocolate pieces. Spread in prepared dish.

Microwave on high 4 to 4-1/2 minutes, turning dish one quarter turn every minute, or until top is slightly dry to touch.

Cool in pan; sift powdered sugar over top, if desired. Cut into bars. Makes 20 to 25.

Banana Crunchies

Chunky pieces of candy provide a crunchy flavor surprise. If you run out of time, substitute a quick sprinkle of powdered sugar for the glaze.

1 banana, peeled and quartered
2/3 cup granulated sugar
1/3 cup margarine or butter
1 egg
1/2 teaspoon ground cinnamon
1/8 teaspoon ground nutmeg
1/4 teaspoon baking soda
1 cup all-purpose flour
1 (2.1-oz.) Butterfinger® candy bar, coarsely chopped

Browned Butter Glaze:
2 tablespoons margarine or butter
1 cup powdered sugar
1/2 teaspoon vanilla extract
1 tablespoon + 1 teaspoon milk

Lightly grease an 8-inch-square microwavable baking dish. In medium bowl, beat banana, sugar, 1/3 cup margarine, egg, cinnamon, nutmeg, soda and flour. Stir in candy. Spread in prepared dish.

Microwave on high 4-1/2 to 5-1/2 minutes turning dish one quarter turn every minute, or until most of top looks dry.

Let stand in dish on flat surface until cool. Spoon glaze over top. Cut into bars. Makes 20 to 25.

Browned Butter Glaze:
In 2-cup microwavable container, microwave 2 tablespoons margarine on high 2-1/2 minutes or until lightly browned. Stir in remaining ingredients.

Cherry-Almond Oatmeal Treats

The slightly chewy bottom layer contrasts with the cherry filling.

1 cup brown sugar, lightly packed
3/4 cup margarine or butter, room temperature
1/4 teaspoon almond extract
1 teaspoon baking powder
1-1/2 cups all-purpose flour
1 cup quick-cooking or old-fashioned rolled oats
2/3 cup cherry preserves
1/4 cup sliced or slivered toasted almonds

In large bowl, beat sugar and margarine until fluffy. Stir in almond extract, baking powder, flour and oats until well mixed but crumbly. Press one-half of mixture in bottom of an 8-inch-square microwavable dish.

Drop tablespoons of preserves into small mounds over top. Sprinkle with remaining flour and oat mixture; then almonds. Microwave on high 7 to 7-1/2 minutes, turning dish a quarter turn after every minute.

Remove from microwave; let stand until lukewarm. Cut into bars or squares. Makes 20 to 25.

8 x 8 cutting guide:

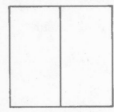 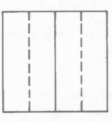

Mississippi Mud Bars

Your microwave helps you make this classic favorite in minutes.

1/3 cup margarine or butter
1 cup granulated sugar
2 tablespoons unsweetened cocoa powder
2 eggs
1 teaspoon vanilla extract
3/4 cup all-purpose flour
1/2 cup flaked coconut
1/4 cup chopped pecans
1/2 cup miniature marshmallows

Frosting:
1/4 cup margarine or butter
3 tablespoons unsweetened cocoa powder
1/2 teaspoon vanilla extract
2-1/2 tablespoons milk
2 cups powdered sugar

Lightly grease an 8-inch-square microwavable baking dish; set aside.
In large microwavable bowl, microwave 1/3 cup margarine on high
1 minute or until melted. Beat in granulated sugar, cocoa, eggs
and 1 teaspoon vanilla extract. Mix in flour, coconut and pecans. Pour
into prepared baking dish. Microwave on high 5 to 5-1/2 minutes,
turning dish a quarter turn after every minute, or until most of top is
dry. Immediately sprinkle marshmallows over top. Let stand on a flat
surface; not on cooling rack. Spread frosting over marshmallows on hot
cake. Cool; cut into bars. Makes 20 to 25.

Frosting:
In medium microwavable bowl, melt 1/4 cup margarine on high
45 seconds. Beat in remaining ingredients.

Chocolate Peanut-Butter Oat Squares

Take advantage of the speed of your microwave to prepare these bars.

2 cups quick-cooking rolled oats
1/2 cup margarine or butter
1/2 cup brown sugar, lightly packed
1/4 cup honey
1/2 cup semi-sweet chocolate pieces
2 tablespoons crunchy peanut butter
2 tablespoons coarsely chopped peanuts

In 6-cup microwavable bowl, combine oats, margarine, brown sugar and honey.

Microwave on high about 2 minutes, stirring once, until margarine melts. Press into an 8-inch-square baking dish.

In 1-cup microwavable measure, combine chocolate pieces and peanut butter. Microwave on high about 1-1/2 minutes or until smooth.

Spread over warm oat mixture. Sprinkle with peanuts. Chill until firm. Cut into squares. Makes 20 to 25.

From a Package Mix

Let package mixes share the work and save you time. There are many cake, cookie, pie and biscuit mixes in your supermarket that enable you to take shortcuts in turning out an unbelievable variety of cookies. Best of all, no one will know that you had a "behind-the-scenes" helper.

Here's the way it works. You can start with a basic cake mix as we did in Upside-Down Coconut-Fruit Squares. We used orange marmalade, flaked coconut and chopped strawberry fruit leather to form a delectable base in the bottom of a baking pan. We topped that with packaged white-cake batter. When baked and turned upside down, we had a pan of exciting, colorful flavors. Cut into squares, it made as many as 48 small servings.

A package of banana-nut muffin mix came to our rescue, resulting in a pineapple-banana Trade-Winds Bar.

A roll of refrigerated sugar-cookie dough formed the base of a real quickie-cookie filled with a chopped chocolate caramel candy bar that's drizzled with chocolate.

For best results, follow the directions given in our recipes. We tested them using the exact combination of products that are indicated.

Brownie Pizza Wedges

Save time with a packaged brownie mix and ready-to-spread fudge frosting, then top with colorful chocolate candies, pecans and cherries.

1 (21.5-oz.) pkg. fudge-brownie mix
1/4 cup water
1/4 cup vegetable oil
1 egg, beaten slightly
1 (16-oz.) container ready-to-spread chocolate fudge frosting
1/2 cup coarsely chopped M & M's®
2 tablespoons coarsely chopped pecans
1/3 cup halved candied cherries

Preheat oven to 350F (175C). Lightly grease a 12-inch pizza pan. In large bowl, combine brownie mix, water, oil and egg. Stir until moistened. Spread on prepared pan.

Bake in preheated oven 22 to 25 minutes or until firm. Cool in pan; spread with frosting. Sprinkle with M & M's, pecans and cherries. Cut into 2-inch wedges. Makes 18 to 20.

Shortcut Cookie Sandwiches

Impress your guests with this incredibly easy treat.

1 (16-oz.) pkg. golden pound-cake mix
1/3 cup margarine or butter, room temperature
1 egg
1 teaspoon grated lemon peel
1/2 teaspoon almond extract
Ready-to-spread chocolate frosting
Powdered sugar

In large bowl, mix dry cake mix, margarine, egg, lemon peel, and almond extract until smooth. Halve dough; form into 2 logs, each about 6 x 1-3/4 inches.

Wrap in plastic wrap or foil; refrigerate at least 2 hours. Preheat oven to 375F (190C). Make 1/4-inch crosswise slices. Place on ungreased cookie sheets.

Bake in preheated oven 7 or 8 minutes or until edges are light brown. Cool slightly; remove to cooling rack. Spread frosting on half the cooled cookies; top with remaining cookies. Sprinkle with powdered sugar. Makes 24 sandwiches.

Tip
Ready-to-spread frosting is available in various flavors. Just open the can, stir with a spoon and spread on half the cooled cookies.

Kaleidoscope Chocolate Crunchies

Bake and cool them in a jelly-roll pan (15 x 10), then they're easy to take to a picnic or potluck in the same pan.

1 (18.25-oz.) pkg. fudge or chocolate-cake mix
1 (8-oz.) carton lowfat vanilla yogurt
1 egg
1/2 cup chopped walnuts
1 cup candy-coated chocolate pieces, coarsely chopped (8 oz.)

Preheat oven to 350F (175C). Grease a 15 x 10-inch jelly-roll pan. In large bowl, combine dry cake mix, yogurt and egg. Mix at low speed until well blended. Stir in nuts. Pour into prepared pan; sprinkle with candy pieces.

Bake in preheated oven 20 to 25 minutes or until set and begins to pull away from sides of pan. Cool in pan. Cut into small squares. Makes 32 to 48.

15 x 10 cutting guide:

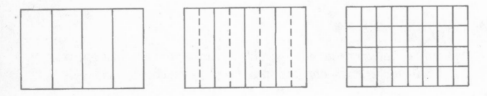

Lemon Drops

For a more festive look, lightly dust them with powdered sugar after they're cool.

1 (18.25-oz.) pkg. moist deluxe lemon-cake mix
1 (8-oz.) carton lowfat lemon yogurt
1 egg, beaten slightly
3/4 cup flaked coconut
1/2 teaspoon grated lemon peel

Preheat oven to 350F (175C). Grease cookie sheets. In large bowl, combine dry cake mix, yogurt and egg; mix until well blended. Stir in coconut and lemon peel.

Drop about 1/2 tablespoon dough at a time, about 2 inches apart, on prepared cookie sheets.

Bake in preheated oven 12 to 14 minutes or until golden. Cool on cookie sheets one minute. Remove from cookie sheets; cool on racks. Makes about 60 to 65.

Chocolate-Glazed Cookie Pizza

This pizza-shaped giant rich cookie can be cut into as many as 36 small wedges, but we prefer to cut it into 24 pieces.

1 refrigerated all-ready uncooked pie crust (1/2 of 15-oz. carton)
1 cup vanilla-wafer crumbs (22 to 24 cookies)
1 teaspoon baking powder
1 (14-oz.) can *sweetened* condensed milk
1/3 cup chopped walnuts or peanuts
3/4 cup candy-coated chocolate pieces

Chocolate Glaze:
1/3 cup semi-sweet chocolate pieces
2 teaspoons vegetable shortening

Preheat oven to 400F (205C). Roll out pie crust to 13 inches. Press in bottom and up sides of ungreased 12-inch pizza pan. Bake in preheated oven 10 minutes.

Meanwhile, combine cookie crumbs, baking powder, and condensed milk. Stir in nuts. Pour over partially baked crust. Sprinkle top with candy.

Bake an additional 14 to 16 minutes or until set. Cool in pan. With tip of teaspoon, drizzle Chocolate Glaze over cooled filling. Cut into thin wedges. Makes 20 to 24.

Chocolate Glaze:
Heat chocolate pieces and shortening; stir until smooth.

Trade-Winds Bars

Take a shortcut to these tropical bars by starting with a muffin mix.

1 (12.5-oz.) pkg. banana-nut muffin mix
1 (8-oz.) can crushed pineapple with juice
1 egg, beaten slightly
1/2 cup chopped macadamia nuts
3 tablespoons caramel ice-cream topping

Preheat oven to 375F (190C). Grease bottom of a 13 x 9-inch baking pan. In large bowl, combine dry muffin mix, pineapple with juice, egg and nuts; stir until well blended. Pour into prepared pan.

Bake in preheated oven 15 to 20 minutes. Cool; drizzle topping over all. Cut into bars. Makes 30 to 40.

13 x 9 cutting guide:

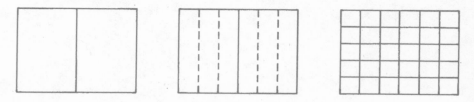

Time-Saver Rounds

Cubes of candy bars make a surprise filling.

3 (2.07-oz.) Snickers® bars
1 (20-oz.) pkg. refrigerated sugar-cookie dough
1/3 cup semi-sweet chocolate, coarsely chopped
2 teaspoons vegetable shortening

Preheat oven to 350F (175C). Cut each candy bar into 8 cubes. Divide dough into 24 equal pieces. Wrap each piece of cookie dough around one piece of candy, forming a ball. Place about 2 inches apart on ungreased cookie sheets.

Bake in preheated oven 10 to 15 minutes or until golden brown. Remove from cookie sheets; cool on racks.

Heat chocolate and shortening until melted. With tip of teaspoon, drizzle melted chocolate over cooled cookies. Makes 24.

Quick Gingerbread Cookies

An easy way to make gingerbread cookies with a distinctive spicy flavor.

1 (14-oz.) pkg. gingerbread mix
1/3 cup applesauce
1/2 cup plain lowfat yogurt
1 tablespoon sugar
1/4 teaspoon ground ginger

Preheat oven to 375F (190C). Lightly grease cookie sheets. In medium bowl, stir gingerbread mix, applesauce and yogurt until smooth.

Drop rounded teaspoon of dough, about 2 inches apart, on prepared cookie sheets. Combine sugar and ginger; sprinkle on tops of unbaked cookies.

Bake in preheated oven 8 to 10 minutes or until firm. Remove from cookie sheets; cool on racks. Makes 38 to 40.

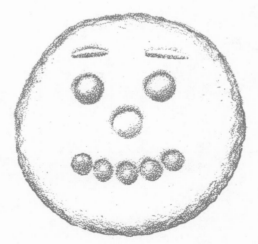

Upside-Down Coconut-Fruit Squares

Check with package directions for mixing cake. Ingredients and methods vary with the kind of mix.

1/2 cup chopped strawberry fruit leather (5 1/2-oz. rolls)
3/4 cup orange marmalade
1/2 cup flaked coconut
3 tablespoons vegetable oil
1 (18.25-oz.) pkg. white or yellow cake mix

Preheat oven to 350F (175C). Generously grease a 15 x 10-inch baking pan. In small bowl, combine fruit leather, marmalade, coconut and 3 tablespoons vegetable oil. Spoon on bottom of prepared pan. Follow package directions for ingredients and mixing cake.

Drop by spoonfuls over coconut mixture in pan.

Bake in preheated oven 27 to 30 minutes or until cake springs back when touched lightly in center. Loosen edges with spatula; immediately invert on tray or large cooling rack. Cool; cut into small squares or bars. Makes 32 to 48.

15 x 10 cutting guide:

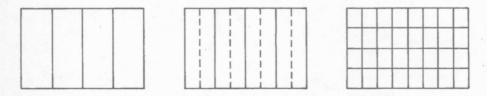

Cherry-Almond Fingers

To form finger-shaped servings, make 3 rows across the short side of the pan, then 12 rows along the long side.

1 (16-oz.) pkg. pound-cake mix
1 egg
1 cup water
1/2 teaspoon almond extract
1 (21-oz.) can cherry-pie filling
1/4 cup toasted sliced almonds

Heat oven to 325F (165C). Grease a 13 x 9-inch baking pan. In medium bowl, beat dry cake mix with egg, water and almond extract 2 to 3 minutes or until smooth. Pour into prepared pan.

Bake in preheated oven 23 to 26 minutes or until top springs back when touched lightly. Cool in pan. Spoon pie filling over cake. Sprinkle with toasted almonds. Cut into 30 finger-shaped pieces. Makes 30.

Coconut-Almond Caramel Strips

A melt-in-the-mouth cookie that's full of goodies and crispy when you take it out of the oven.

1 (16-oz.) pkg. golden pound-cake mix
1 egg
1/3 cup margarine or butter, room temperature
1/2 teaspoon almond extract
1/2 cup sliced almonds
1/2 cup flaked coconut
1/4 cup caramel or butterscotch ice-cream topping

Preheat oven to 350F (175C). Grease a large cookie sheet. In large bowl, combine dry cake mix, egg, margarine and almond extract. Mix at low speed until smooth.

Divide dough into 4 equal parts. On prepared cookie sheet, pat or roll out 2 quarters of dough each into a strip 2 inches wide and 15 inches long. Sprinkle tops with sliced almonds and coconut. Drizzle ice cream topping over each strip.

Bake in preheated oven 12 to 14 minutes or until lightly browned. Cool on cookie sheet about 2 minutes. While still warm, cut crosswise into 1-inch strips. Remove from cookie sheet; cool on racks. Repeat with remaining dough. Makes about 62 to 66.

Macadamia White-Chocolate Cookies

Thanks to the cake mix, you can produce a large number of memorable cookies in a short time.

1 (18.25-oz.) pkg. German chocolate-cake mix
1 cup lowfat plain yogurt
1 egg
1-1/2 cups vanilla-milk or white-chocolate pieces (9- or 10-oz.)
1/2 cup coarsely chopped macadamia nuts

Preheat oven to 350F (175C). In large bowl, combine dry cake mix, yogurt and egg. Beat until smooth. Stir in vanilla-milk pieces and macadamia nuts.

Drop by rounded teaspoons on ungreased cookie sheets.

Bake in preheated oven 10 to 12 minutes. Cool 1 minute. Remove from cookie sheets; cool on racks. Makes 68 to 72.

Spicy Butterscotch Drops

Start with spice-cake mix for a speedy way to produce homemade cookies within a few minutes.

1 (18.25-oz.) pkg. spice-cake mix
2 eggs
1/3 cup vegetable oil
1 cup quick-cooking rolled oats
1 cup butterscotch chips

Preheat oven to 350F (175C). In large mixing bowl, mix dry spice-cake mix, eggs and oil until well blended. Stir in oats and chips.

Drop by teaspoons 2 inches apart on ungreased cookie sheets.

Bake in preheated oven 10 to 12 minutes or until edges turn golden. Cool on cookie sheet one minute. Remove to cooling racks. Makes 66 to 72.

Short-Order Chocolate-Mint Wedges

These individually wrapped rectangular candies consist of three alternate layers of minty green and rich chocolate flavors.

1 stick or 1/2 of (11-oz.) pkg. pie-crust mix
1 tablespoon dark-brown sugar
2 tablespoons plus 2 teaspoons water
28 chocolate mint or crème de menthe
    wafers (4.67-oz.package), coarsley chopped
1/4 cup chopped walnuts

Preheat oven to 425F (220C). In medium bowl, crumble pie-crust mix. Add sugar and water. Form into a ball. Pat out on bottom of ungreased 9-inch-round cake pan.

Bake in preheated oven 14 or 15 minutes or until golden. Remove from oven; immediately sprinkle with chopped mints. Return to oven 1 minute. Carefully swirl chocolate with spatula; sprinkle with nuts. Cool; cut into wedges. Makes 12 to 15.

Almond Bites

Save time by using a refrigerated sugar-cookie dough; decorate with colored sugar compatible with your color scheme.

1 (20-oz.) pkg. refrigerated sugar-cookie dough
1 (7-oz.) pkg. almond paste
Colored sugar or nonpareils

Preheat oven to 350F (175C). Cut cookie dough in half lengthwise; then half again crosswise to make 4 equal pieces. On floured board, pat or roll each quarter to a 16 x 2-1/2-inch rectangle.

Divide almond paste into 4 equal parts. Shape each into a rope 16 inches long. Place a rope down the center of each dough rectangle. Bring edges of dough up and over almond-paste rope so edges overlap slightly; press lightly. Cut crosswise into 1-inch pieces. Place seam-side down on cookie sheets. Sprinkle with colored sugar or nonpareils.

Bake in preheated oven 9 or 10 minutes. Remove from cookie sheets; cool on racks. Makes about 64.

Hand-shaped Goodies

There's an unlimited number of shapes and textures for cookies, shaped by patting or rolling dough with your hands. None of these shapes require molds, rolling pins or time-consuming cookie cutters.

Shape them into rounds resembling mini-snowballs, pat them into sugar-coated strips, make them into crunchy rounds encircled with coconut or encase them in tiny crinkled-paper cups.

If dough is sticky, sprinkle your hands with a little flour before handling it. To form a small ball of dough, roll the designated amount between the palms of your hands. Then roll into chopped nuts or powdered sugar, if desired. When the recipe indicates that it should be flattened, lightly press top of ball with a flat-bottom glass. If the glass sticks to the dough, dip glass in granulated sugar or lightly grease the bottom before using it.

Peanut-butter cookies have a traditional design created by a fork. Just press fork tines on top of round of dough in two directions, creating a crisscross pattern.

The charm of the ever-popular Chocolate Crinkles is created by the crackled chocolate designs peeking out of the top between patches of powdered sugar.

Traditional Snickerdoodles

Favorite old-fashioned cookie with cinnamon-sugar coating with a crackled look.

3/4 cup sugar
1/2 cup margarine or butter, room temperature
1 egg
1/2 teaspoon vanilla extract
1 teaspoon cream of tartar
1/2 teaspoon baking soda
1-1/2 cups all-purpose flour

Topping:
2 tablespoons sugar
1 teaspoon ground cinnamon

Preheat oven to 375F (190C). In large bowl, beat 3/4 cup sugar, margarine, egg, vanilla extract, cream of tartar, soda and flour until a smooth dough is formed.

Shape into 1-inch balls. Roll in topping. Place 2 inches apart on ungreased cookie sheets.

Bake in preheated oven 8 to 10 minutes or until golden. Remove from cookie sheets; cool on racks. Makes 38 to 40.

Topping:
In small bowl, combine 2 tablespoons sugar and cinnamon.

Tip
Lightly sprinkle your hands with flour before making balls of dough.

Mini-Snowballs

*For a snowball effect, remove cookies from oven as soon as they begin to
brown, then coat with powdered sugar until they are white.*

3/4 cup margarine or butter
1/3 cup powdered sugar
1 teaspoon vanilla extract
1-1/2 cups all-purpose flour
1/4 cup powdered sugar for coating

Preheat oven to 350F (175C). In medium mixing bowl, beat margarine,
1/3 cup powdered sugar and vanilla extract until fluffy. Stir in flour.

Pinch off a heaping teaspoon of dough; roll gently between palms to
form balls about 1-inch in diameter. Bake about 1-inch apart on
ungreased cookie sheets.

Bake in preheated oven 13 to 15 minutes or until bottoms begin to
turn golden. Remove from cookies sheets. Roll in 1/4 cup powdered
sugar while warm. Cool on racks. Roll in sugar again when cool.
Makes 35 to 40.

Super-Size Ginger Disks

A time-saving way to make large-size spicy rounds with a harmonious blend of spices that appeals to the most critical cookie lover.

1/4 cup molasses
3/4 cup brown sugar, lightly packed
1/2 cup vegetable oil
1 egg
2 cups all-purpose flour
1 teaspoon baking soda
1 teaspoon ground ginger
1/4 teaspoon ground nutmeg
1/2 teaspoon ground cinnamon
Granulated sugar

Preheat oven to 350F (175C). In large bowl, beat molasses, brown sugar, vegetable oil, egg, flour, baking soda and spices until smooth.

Shape 1/4 cup dough into a 2-inch ball. Roll in granulated sugar. Place about 3 inches apart on ungreased cookie sheet. Flatten slightly to 2-1/2 to 3 inches. Repeat procedure with remaining dough.

Bake in preheated oven 15 to 17 minutes or until edges are set. Remove from cookie sheet; cool on rack. Makes 8 to 9 (4-inch) cookies.

Crunchy Sesame Balls

Crispy toasted sesame seeds lend an Oriental flavor.

1 egg
2/3 cup sugar
1/3 cup margarine or butter, room temperature
1 teaspoon vanilla extract
1/2 teaspoon baking powder
1-1/3 cups all-purpose flour
1/2 cup toasted sesame seeds

Preheat oven to 350F (175C). In medium bowl, beat egg, sugar, margarine and vanilla extract until smooth. Beat in baking powder and flour.

Form dough into 1-inch balls. Roll each in sesame seeds. Place about 1-inch apart on ungreased cookie sheets.

Bake in preheated oven 12 to 15 minutes or until firm. Remove from cookie sheets; cool on rack. Makes about 35.

Tip
Toast sesame seeds in a shallow baking dish in 350F (175C) oven about 5 to 7 minutes or until golden brown.

Brazil-Nut Crescents

The food processor is a speedy way to chop nuts and mix dough.

3/4 cup Brazil nuts
1-1/2 cups all-purpose flour
2/3 cup powdered sugar
1 teaspoon vanilla extract
3/4 cup margarine or butter
1/3 cup powdered sugar for coating

In food processor, finely chop nuts. Add flour, 2/3 cup sugar, vanilla extract and margarine. Process until well blended and crumbly. Preheat oven to 375F (190C).

Form one tablespoon dough in a ball. With fingers, roll into a 3-inch log; place on ungreased cookie sheets and slightly curve each log to form a crescent shape. Repeat with remaining dough.

Bake in preheated oven 10 to 12 minutes or until set but not brown. Remove from cookie sheets; cool on racks about 3 minutes. Roll in powdered sugar while still warm but not hot. Makes about 32.

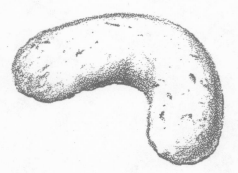

S'Mores Special

An updated version of a childhood favorite that combines marshmallows and chocolate.

1-1/2 cups all-purpose flour
1 teaspoon baking powder
1 egg, beaten slightly
3/4 cup sugar
1 teaspoon vanilla extract
1/2 cup margarine or butter, room temperature
1 cup miniature marshmallows
1 (4-oz.) milk-chocolate candy bar, broken into small pieces

Preheat oven to 350F (175C). In large bowl, combine flour, baking powder, egg, sugar, vanilla extract and margarine. Beat until smooth.

Pat dough in bottom of an ungreased 9-inch cake pan. Sprinkle top with marshmallows, then chocolate pieces.

Bake in preheated oven 32 to 34 minutes or until golden brown. Cool in pan. Cut into thin wedges. Makes 12 to 16.

Express Cashew-Orange Balls

A hint of orange combines nicely with the richness of the cashews.

1/2 cup cashew nuts
1/2 cup margarine or butter, chilled and cut into 8 pieces
1/3 cup granulated sugar
1 teaspoon grated orange peel
1 cup all-purpose flour
1/4 teaspoon ground nutmeg
2 tablespoons sifted powdered sugar or 1 oz. melted semi-sweet
  chocolate

Preheat oven to 350F (175C). Combine cashews, margarine, granulated sugar, orange peel, flour and nutmeg in food processor. Process until mixture begins to form a ball.

Remove from processor; form into 1-inch balls. Place balls about 1 inch apart on ungreased cookie sheets.

Bake in preheated oven about 20 minutes or until firm. Remove from cookie sheets; cool on racks. Sift powdered sugar over cookies or dip tops of cookies into melted chocolate. Makes 30 to 32.

Tip:
Use your food processor for quick and easy mixing of these cookies.

Mini-Brownie Cups

Treat yourself, have one or two of these tantalizing morsels.

2 oz. unsweetened chocolate
1/4 cup margarine or butter
2 eggs
1 cup sugar
1/2 teaspoon vanilla extract
1/2 cup all-purpose flour
1/4 cup chopped pecans or walnuts

Fudge Frosting:
2 tablespoons margarine or butter
1 oz. unsweetened chocolate
2-1/2 cups powdered sugar
3 tablespoons milk

Insert a bon-bon paper liner in each mini-muffin pan; set aside. In small saucepan, melt chocolate and margarine over low heat; set aside. Preheat oven to 350F (175C). In medium mixing bowl, whisk eggs, sugar and vanilla extract until well blended. Stir in melted-chocolate mixture; then flour and nuts. Spoon 1 level tablespoon into each small, paper-lined muffin cup. Bake in preheated oven 15 minutes or until firm. Remove from muffin cups; cool in paper liners. Top each with frosting. Makes 28 to 30.

Fudge Frosting:
In medium saucepan, over low heat, melt margarine and chocolate. Remove from heat. Stir in powdered sugar and milk.

Honey Cardamom Crinkles

Slightly crunchy edges encircle soft cake-like centers.

1/4 cup honey
1 egg, beaten slightly
3/4 cup sugar
2/3 cup vegetable oil
1-1/2 teaspoons baking soda
2-1/4 cups all-purpose flour
1/2 teaspoon ground cardamom
3 tablespoons sugar for coating

Preheat oven to 350F (175C). In large bowl, mix honey, egg, sugar and vegetable oil until well blended. Stir in soda, flour and cardamom.

Form into 1-inch balls between palms. Roll in coating sugar. Place 2 inches apart on ungreased cookie sheets.

Bake in preheated oven 10 to 12 minutes or until golden. Remove from cookie sheets; cool on racks. Makes about 50.

Fruit Diagonals

A lemon glaze is drizzled over these colorful fruit bars.

1/2 cup margarine or butter, room temperature
3/4 cup sugar
1 egg
1 cup all-purpose flour
1 teaspoon baking soda
1/2 cup mixed finely chopped candied fruits
3/4 cup quick-cooking rolled oats

Glaze:
1 tablespoon margarine or butter
1 cup powdered sugar
1 - 2 tablespoons lemon juice

Preheat oven to 350F (175C). In large mixing bowl, beat margarine and sugar until fluffy. Beat in egg, flour and soda. Stir in candied fruits and oats. Divide dough into six sections. Place 2 sections about 4 inches apart in an ungreased 15 x 10-inch baking pan. Pat each section into strips about 9 inches long and 2 inches wide. Repeat with remaining strips. Bake in preheated oven 15 to 16 minutes or until firm. Cool in pan 2 minutes; then cut each strip into 1-inch diagonal bars and completely cool in pan. With a teaspoon, drizzle glaze in zig-zag pattern over cooled cookies. Makes 40 to 50 strips.

Glaze:
In a small bowl, combine margarine or butter, powdered sugar and lemon juice.

Lacy Cup Cookies

If baked cookies on cookie sheet are difficult to remove, reheat them in the oven a minute or two.

1/4 cup margarine or butter
2 tablespoons light corn syrup
1/3 cup brown sugar, lightly packed
1/2 cup all-purpose flour
2 tablespoons finely chopped pecans
1/4 teaspoon ground cinnamon
Frozen yogurt or ice cream

Preheat oven to 375F (190C). Lightly grease cookie sheet. In medium saucepan, melt margarine with corn syrup and brown sugar. Remove from heat; stir in flour, pecans and cinnamon.

Drop two level tablespoons for each, about 4 inches apart, on prepared cookie sheet.

Bake in preheated oven 5 to 8 minutes until golden brown. Let stand on cookie sheet about 1 minute or until edges are firm. With wide spatula, transfer to inverted custard cup; cool. Fill each with a scoop of frozen yogurt or ice cream. Serve immediately. Makes 6.

Fruit Cake Miniatures

You will need about 35 paper liners for bite-size cakes.

1/2 cup vegetable oil
1/2 cup brown sugar, lightly packed
1 egg
1 cup all-purpose flour
1/2 teaspoon baking soda
1 teaspoon ground cinnamon
1/4 teaspoon ground cloves
1 cup mixed chopped candied fruits
1/2 cup chopped walnuts
Red or green candied cherry halves, if desired

Insert a bon-bon paper liner in each mini-muffin pan; set aside. Preheat oven to 375F (190C). In large bowl, beat oil, brown sugar and egg until well blended. Beat in flour, soda, cinnamon and cloves. Stir in fruits and walnuts.

Spoon about 1 level tablespoon mixture into each paper-lined muffin pan. Top each with half a candied cherry, if desired.

Bake in preheated oven 10 to 12 minutes or until firm. Cool in pan. Makes 34 to 36.

Apricot-Pineapple Wedges

Healthful cookies crammed full of yogurt and fruit.

3/4 cup whole-wheat flour
3/4 cup all-purpose flour
1/2 cup margarine or butter, room temperature
1/3 cup brown sugar, lightly packed
1/2 cup granulated sugar
1 cup apricot-pineapple yogurt (8 oz.)
2 eggs, beaten slightly
1/2 cup chopped dried apricots

Preheat oven to 350F (175C). With pastry blender or fork, mix whole-wheat and all-purpose flour, margarine and brown sugar until crumbly. Set aside 1 cup crumbly mixture.

Press remaining crumbs in bottom of an ungreased 9-inch round cake pan. Bake in preheated oven 20 minutes.

In medium bowl, combine granulated sugar, yogurt, eggs and apricots. Spoon over baked crust. Sprinkle with reserved crumb mixture.

Bake an additional 25 minutes or until pick inserted in center comes out clean. Cool in pan. Cut into thin wedges. Makes about 16.

Bayou Mini-Cups

The wonderful flavors of pralines result in a memorable treat.

Crust:
1/2 cup margarine or butter, room temperature
1 (3-oz.) pkg. cream cheese, room temperature
1 cup all-purpose flour

Filling:
2 eggs, beaten slightly
1/2 cup dark corn syrup
1/3 cup brown sugar, lightly packed
1/4 cup all-purpose flour
1 teaspoon vanilla extract
1/2 cup chopped pecans
1/4 cup flaked coconut

Crust:
Preheat oven to 350F (175C). In medium bowl, beat margarine, cream cheese and 1 cup flour until well blended. Divide mixture into 24 pieces.

Press into bottom and sides of ungreased mini-muffin pans. Spoon about 1 tablespoon filling into each pastry-lined pan.

Bake in preheated oven 25 to 30 minutes or until crust is golden. Let stand in pan 3 minutes. Remove and cool on rack. Makes 24.

Filling:
Mix eggs, corn syrup, brown sugar, 1/4 cup flour and vanilla extract until smooth. Stir in pecans and coconut.

Crunchy Fruit Rolls

They're crunchy on the outside, with date centers that have a hint of orange flavor.

1/2 cup margarine or butter, room temperature
1/3 cup brown sugar, lightly packed
1 egg
1-1/3 cups all-purpose flour
1/2 cup chopped dates
1 teaspoon grated orange peel
3/4 cup natural wheat and barley cereal nuggets

Preheat oven to 350F (175C). In medium bowl, beat margarine, sugar and egg. Stir in flour; then dates and orange peel.

With fingers, lightly roll about 1 tablespoon dough at a time, into a cylinder about 2 inches long. Roll each in cereal. Place 1-inch apart on ungreased cookie sheet.

Bake in preheated oven 10 to 12 minutes. Remove from cookie sheet; cool on rack. Makes 24 to 26.

Sugar & Spice Strips

Sparkling grains of crystal sugar give these cookies a festive look.

1 cup brown sugar, lightly packed
1/4 cup molasses
1 egg
1/2 cup vegetable oil
1/2 teaspoon ground ginger
1/2 teaspoon ground allspice
1/2 teaspoon ground nutmeg
1-1/2 teaspoons baking soda
2 cups all-purpose flour
1 tablespoon granulated or crystal sugar

In large bowl, beat brown sugar, molasses, egg and oil until smooth.
Beat in spices, soda and flour. Preheat oven to 350F (175C).

Divide dough into four pieces. On large ungreased cookie sheets, pat
two quarters into 15 x 3-inch strips; sprinkle with granulated or crystal
sugar. Repeat with remaining two quarters of dough on another cookie
sheet.

Bake in preheated oven 10 to 12 minutes or until lightly browned.
Cool on cookie sheets 2 or 3 minutes. While warm, cut crosswise into
1-inch strips and cool on rack. Makes about 55 to 60.

Jeweled Shortbread Wedges

Vary the flavor of filling to suit your taste. Strawberry and apricot preserves are other favorites.

1/2 cup margarine or butter, room temperature
1/4 cup brown sugar, lightly packed
1 cup all-purpose flour
1/2 teaspoon vanilla extract
1/4 cup grape or apple jelly
2 tablespoons toasted slivered almonds

Preheat oven to 350F (175C). In medium bowl, mix margarine, sugar, flour and vanilla extract until smooth. Pat into bottom of an ungreased 8-inch-round cake pan.

Bake in preheated oven 20 minutes or until light golden brown. Lightly spread with jelly. Sprinkle with almonds. Completely cool in pan; cut into wedges. Makes 16.

Fresh Ginger Rounds

For spicy cookies, increase the ginger to 1 tablespoon.

3/4 cup margarine or butter, room temperature
1 cup brown sugar, lightly packed
1 egg
2 tablespoons molasses
1-1/2 teaspoons peeled, grated, fresh ginger
1 teaspoon baking soda
2-1/4 cups all-purpose flour

Preheat oven to 350F (175C). In large bowl, beat margarine, brown sugar, egg and molasses until smooth. Add grated ginger, soda and flour; beat until well mixed.

Form into 1-1/4 inch balls. Place 2 inches apart on ungreased cookie sheets.

Bake in preheated oven 10 to 12 minutes or until set. Remove from cookie sheets; cool on racks. Makes 43 to 45.

Tip
Fresh ginger is a smooth, tan, gnarled root that resembles an elongated potato. To use it in this recipe, peel and finely grate before measuring.

Chocolate Crinkles

The chocolate center peeks out from the powdered-sugar coating.

1/2 cup vegetable oil
1 cup granulated sugar
1 egg
1 teaspoon vanilla extract
2 tablespoons milk
1/4 cup unsweetened cocoa powder
1 teaspoon baking powder
1/2 teaspoon baking soda
2 cups all-purpose flour
1/3 cup powdered sugar

Preheat oven to 350F (175C). In large bowl, beat oil, 1 cup granulated sugar, egg, vanilla extract, milk, cocoa, baking powder, baking soda and flour.

Form into 1-1/4 inch balls; roll in powdered sugar. Place about 3 inches apart on ungreased cookie sheets.

Bake in preheated oven 10 to 12 minutes or until firm on edges. Remove from cookie sheets; cool on racks. Makes about 35.

Favorite Peanut-Butter Cookies

The familiar crisscross pattern tells you these are peanut-butter goodies.

1/2 cup granulated sugar
1/2 cup brown sugar, lightly packed
1/2 cup peanut butter
1/2 cup margarine or butter, room temperature
1 egg
1/2 teaspoon baking soda
1-1/2 cups all-purpose flour
1/2 teaspoon vanilla extract

Preheat oven to 375F(190C). In large bowl, beat all ingredients until well blended.

Shape into 1-inch balls. Place 2 inches apart on ungreased cookie sheets. Lightly press dough with fork tines, creating a crisscross pattern. If fork sticks, dip in granulated sugar.

Bake in preheated oven 9 to 11 minutes or until golden. Remove from cookie sheets; cool on racks. Makes 48 to 52.

Bake-a-Bar

Busy cooks love bar cookies. There's no rolling out dough, cutting elaborate and fancy shapes or tedious decorating. Just mix everything together, pour and bake it.

There's a difference of opinion regarding finishing touches on these cookies. Those who enjoy a specific flavor may prefer the bar without any adornment. On the other extreme, there's the cookie lover who demands a thick layer of dark-chocolate frosting over all. We have provided a variety of quick ideas ranging from a plain unadorned bar or a quick dusting of powdered sugar to a variety of easy drizzles and glazes.

Bars are the good old standbys in the cookie world. Just bake them, let them cool in the pan and then cover with foil or plastic wrap. Transport them in the pan in which they were baked and they arrive at picnics or potlucks in peak condition. Cut bars or squares just before serving.

8-inch square . . . . .20 to 25 bars or squares
11 x 7-inch rectangle . . . . . .22 to 32 bars or squares
9-inch square . . . . .24 to 32 bars or squares
13 x 9-inch rectangle . . . . . .30 to 40 bars or squares
15 x 10-inch rectangle . . . . .32 to 48 bars or squares

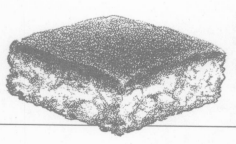

Swirled Peanut-Butter Brownies

Double your pleasure with brownies swirled with peanut-butter batter.

4 eggs
1-3/4 cups sugar
1 teaspoon vanilla extract
1/2 cup vegetable oil
1-1/4 cups all-purpose flour
1/2 teaspoon baking powder
1/3 cup unsweetened cocoa powder
1 cup peanut-butter pieces

Preheat oven to 350F (175C). Grease a 13 x 9-inch baking pan. In large mixing bowl, beat eggs, sugar, vanilla extract, oil, flour and baking powder.

Pour 1/2 mixture (or about 1-1/2 cups) into medium bowl. Add cocoa to mixture in medium bowl. With a tablespoon, drop mounds of cocoa batter about an inch apart into bottom of prepared pan. Add peanut-butter pieces to remaining batter.

Drop mounds of peanut-butter batter on top of chocolate mixture. Use spatula to gently swirl batters into marbled effect.

Bake in preheated oven 30 to 33 minutes or until edges begin to leave side of pan. Cool in pan. Cut in squares. Makes 30 to 40.

Minute-Maker Sweeties

Indulge yourself and enjoy several of these delectables.

1/4 cup margarine or butter
1-1/2 cups macaroon-cookie crumbs (5-1/2 oz.)
1 (14-oz.) can *sweetened* condensed milk
1 (6-oz.) pkg. diced mixed dried fruits and raisins
1 (10-oz.) pkg. vanilla-milk or white-chocolate chips

Preheat oven to 350F (175C). Melt margarine in a 13 x 9-inch baking pan. Make a layer of all the macaroon crumbs; pour condensed milk over crumbs. Top with a layer of dried fruits; then with a layer of chips. Do not stir.

Bake in preheated oven 20 to 22 minutes or until edges are golden. Cool completely in pan. Cut into bars. Makes about 35 to 40.

Tip
Let the margarine or butter melt in baking pan while preheating the oven. Remove pan from oven, then add layers of other ingredients and bake.

Hurry-Up Chocolate-Chip Cookies

Another version of our family's favorite snack.

1/4 cup granulated sugar
2/3 cup brown sugar, lightly packed
1/2 cup butter-flavored vegetable oil
1 egg
1 teaspoon vanilla extract
1/2 teaspoon baking soda
1-1/2 cups all-purpose flour
1 (6-oz.) pkg. semi-sweet chocolate pieces

Cut parchment or wax paper into a 9 x 11-inch piece. Line bottom and 1-inch up two sides of a 9-inch-square baking pan. Preheat oven to 375F (190C). In large bowl, beat sugars, oil, egg and vanilla extract until smooth. Stir in baking soda and flour.

Spread in prepared pan; lightly press with back of spoon to make it even. Sprinkle chocolate pieces over top. Lightly press into dough.

Bake in preheated oven 24 to 26 minutes; cool in pan 5 minutes. Gently lift out of pan by holding edges of parchment or waxed paper. Make 2 crosswise cuts about 3-inches apart across the cookies. Then make 7 vertical cuts in the opposite direction. Makes 24.

Cherry Sour-Cream Squares

To keep these eye-appealing squares longer than 2 or 3 hours, cover and hide them in the refrigerator.

1-1/2 cups all-purpose flour
1/4 cup powdered sugar
1/2 cup margarine or butter
1/2 cup cherry preserves
1 egg, beaten slightly
1/2 cup dairy sour cream
2 tablespoons brown sugar
1/2 teaspoon vanilla extract

Preheat oven to 350F (175C). In medium bowl, combine flour, powdered sugar and margarine. Using a pastry blender or fork, blend until mixture resembles coarse crumbs. Press on bottom of an ungreased 9-inch-square baking pan.

Bake in preheated oven 19 to 20 minutes or until edges begin to brown. Remove from oven; immediately spread preserves over top.

Mix egg, sour cream, brown sugar and vanilla extract. Spoon over preserves. Return pan to oven; bake 19 to 20 minutes or until topping is firm. Cool in pan; cut into squares or bars. Makes 24 to 30.

Spicy Pecan Crisps

Three spices accent these nutty morsels.

3/4 cup brown sugar, lightly packed
3/4 cup butter-flavored vegetable shortening
1 egg yolk
1/4 teaspoon ground cardamom
1/4 teaspoon ground ginger
1 teaspoon ground cinnamon
1-3/4 cups all-purpose flour
1 egg white, beaten slightly
1/2 cup pecans, chopped

Preheat oven to 350F (175C). In large bowl, beat brown sugar, butter-flavored shortening and egg yolk until light. Beat in cardamom, ginger, cinnamon and flour.

Pat into an ungreased 15 x 10-inch jelly-roll pan. Brush with egg white. Sprinkle with pecans.

Bake in preheated oven 20 to 24 minutes or until golden brown. Cool in pan. Break into irregular-size pieces. Makes 25 to 30 pieces.

Tip
To spread dough in the pan, just pat it with your fingers until it's evenly distributed.

White-Chocolate Brownies

Creamy colored and filled with white chocolate.

5 oz. vanilla-milk chips or white-chocolate pieces
1/4 cup margarine or butter
1/2 cup all-purpose flour
2 eggs
3/4 cup sugar
1/2 teaspoon vanilla extract
1/2 cup chopped cashew nuts

Preheat oven to 350F (175C). Grease an 8-inch-square baking pan. In medium saucepan, melt vanilla-milk chips and margarine over low heat. Remove from heat. Beat in flour, eggs, sugar and vanilla extract. Stir in cashews.

Bake in preheated oven 25 to 30 minutes or until edges begin to leave sides of pan. Cool in pan. Cut into squares. Makes 20 to 25.

> **Tip:**
> *Save time by putting the vanilla-milk chips and margarine in a microwavable bowl and melting in your microwave oven.*

8 x 8 cutting guide:

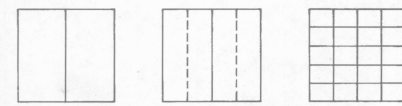

Orange-Chiffon Bars

Flavor and texture resemble a miniature orange-chiffon cake.

2 eggs
1/2 cup vegetable oil
1 cup sugar
1/2 teaspoon baking powder
3/4 cup all-purpose flour
1/2 teaspoon grated orange peel
1 tablespoon orange-flavored liqueur

Preheat oven to 350F (175C). Grease a 9-inch-square baking pan. In medium bowl, beat eggs, oil, sugar, baking powder and flour until smooth. Stir in orange peel and liqueur. Pour into prepared pan.

Bake in preheated oven 25 to 30 minutes or until golden brown. Cool in pan. Cut into squares or bars. Makes 24 to 32.

9 x 9 cutting guide:

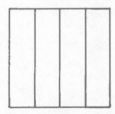

Celebration Bars

Let's celebrate every day with a cookie.

1-1/2 cups chocolate-fudge cookies, crushed (about 18)
1/4 cup margarine or butter, melted
1 cup (6-oz.) vanilla-milk or white-chocolate pieces
1/3 cup sugar
1 (8-oz.) pkg. Neufchatel cheese, room temperature
3 eggs
1/2 teaspoon vanilla extract
2 tablespoons Crème de Cacao

Preheat oven to 350F (175C). In small bowl, combine crushed cookies and margarine. Press on bottom of an ungreased 9-inch-square baking pan; sprinkle with vanilla-milk pieces.

In medium bowl, beat sugar and cheese until smooth; add eggs, vanilla extract and Crème de Cacao, mixing until well combined. Carefully pour over chips.

Bake in preheated oven 25 to 30 minutes or until firm. Thoroughly cool in pan before cutting. Makes 24 to 32 bars.

Tip
For ease in cutting, chill; then refrigerate until serving time.

Many-Layered Temptations

All the layers blend together to produce a mouth-watering candy-like creation.

1/4 cup margarine or butter
24 or 25 crushed vanilla wafers (about 1 cup)
1 (12-oz.) pkg. butterscotch pieces
3/4 cup flaked coconut
1 (12-oz.) pkg. vanilla-milk or white-chocolate pieces
1 egg, slightly beaten
1/4 cup milk
1/4 cup all-purpose flour
1/2 cup finely chopped blanched almonds

Preheat oven to 325F (165C). Melt margarine in a 13 x 9-inch baking pan in oven 4 to 5 minutes. Top with crushed vanilla wafers; then butterscotch pieces and coconut.

In small bowl, combine vanilla-milk pieces, egg, milk and flour.

Drop by spoonfuls over coconut; spread carefully. Sprinkle with almonds.

Bake 25 to 30 minutes. Cool in pan. Cut into bars. Makes 30 to 40.

Maple-Walnut Cheesecake Tempters

Three-layer bars that are well worth your time and effort.

1/3 cup brown sugar, lightly packed
1/3 cup margarine or butter
1 cup all-purpose flour
1/2 cup chopped walnuts
1 (8-oz.) pkg. Neufchatel cheese, room temperature
2 eggs
1/2 cup maple syrup

Preheat oven to 350F (175C). In medium bowl, beat brown sugar and margarine until fluffy. Stir in flour and walnuts until mixture resembles crumbs. Set aside 3/4 cup crumb mixture.

Firmly press remaining crumbs in bottom of an ungreased 9-inch-square baking pan. Bake in preheated oven 14 to 16 minutes.

In medium bowl, beat cheese until smooth. Mix in eggs and maple syrup. Spread over baked crust. Sprinkle reserved crumbs over top. Bake an additional 22 to 24 minutes. Cool; cut into bars. Refrigerate, if kept more than 2 or 3 hours. Makes 24 to 32.

Bits-of-Gold Bars

Flecks of carrot brighten the bars.

2 eggs, slightly beaten
1/2 cup vegetable oil
3/4 cup sugar
1-1/2 cups all-purpose flour
1/2 teaspoon ground cinnamon
1 teaspoon baking powder
1/2 teaspoon baking soda
1 cup grated carrots
1/3 cup orange juice
1/4 cup finely chopped pecans

Topping:
2 cups powdered sugar
1/4 cup margarine or butter
2 teaspoons lemon juice
1 tablespoon milk

Preheat oven to 350F (175C). Grease a 15 x 10-inch jelly-roll pan. In large bowl, combine eggs, oil and sugar. Stir in flour, cinnamon, baking powder, soda, carrots, orange juice, and pecans. Pour into prepared pan. Bake in preheated oven 15 to 20 minutes or until top springs back when lightly pressed with finger. Cool in pan.

Spread topping on cooled cake. Cut into bars. Makes 35 to 40.

Topping:
In a small bowl, beat ingredients until smooth.

> ### Tip
> *Save time and energy by grating carrots in a food processor. It takes one very large or two medium carrots for this recipe.*

Chocolate Date Quickies

Dates impart an extra richness.

2 cups finely crushed graham-cracker crumbs (about 20 crackers)
1 (6-oz.) pkg. semi-sweet chocolate pieces
1 (14-oz.) can *sweetened* condensed milk
3/4 cup chopped dates
1/2 cup chopped walnuts

Preheat oven to 350F (175C). Grease an 8-inch-square baking pan. In medium bowl, combine graham cracker crumbs, chocolate pieces and condensed milk. Stir in chopped dates and walnuts. Spread in prepared pan.

Bake in preheated oven 25 to 30 minutes. Cool in pan; then cut into bars. Makes 20 to 25.

Tip
To save time, buy a box of graham-cracker crumbs instead of crushing your own.

Oat Shortbread

A flaky, delicately flavored cookie reminiscent of olden days.

1/2 cup all-purpose flour
1/2 cup brown sugar, lightly packed
2 cups old-fashioned or quick-cooking rolled oats
1 teaspoon vanilla extract
2/3 cup margarine or butter, melted

Preheat oven to 350F (175C). In large bowl, combine flour, brown sugar and oats. Add vanilla extract and melted margarine. Stir until well mixed. Press on bottom of an ungreased 9-inch-square baking pan.

Bake in preheated oven 18 to 20 minutes or until golden. Cool in pan. Cut into bars. Makes 24 to 32.

9 x 9 cutting guide:

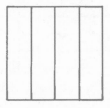

Pronto Muesli Coconut Squares

Apple-and-almond muesli is compatible with other flavors in this cookie.

1/4 cup margarine or butter
3 cups muesli (with apples and almonds)
1/2 cup flaked coconut
1/2 cup sliced almonds
1 (14-oz.) can *sweetened* condensed milk

Preheat oven to 325F (165C). Put margarine in a 13 x 9-inch baking pan. Heat in oven 4 to 5 minutes, or until margarine melts. Remove from oven; top with muesli. Sprinkle with coconut and almonds. Pour condensed milk over all.

Bake in preheated oven 23 to 25 minutes or until golden. Cool; cut into squares. Makes 30 to 40.

13 x 9 cutting guide:

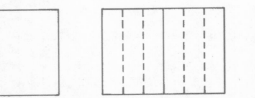

Island Bars

Make the most of your food processor, save chopping and mixing time.

1/2 cup macadamia nuts
1/4 cup flaked coconut
1-1/4 cups all-purpose flour
1/2 cup brown sugar, lightly packed
1/2 cup margarine or butter, chilled and cubed
1/2 cup apricot-pineapple jam

Preheat oven to 350F (175C). In food processor, combine nuts, coconut, flour, brown sugar and chilled margarine. Process until mixture is texture of coarse crumbs. Remove 1/2 cup crumb mixture. Press remaining in bottom of an ungreased 9-inch-square baking pan.

Bake in preheated oven 18 minutes. Remove from oven. Carefully spread jam over crust; sprinkle top with remaining crumbs. Return to oven; bake another 20 minutes or until golden. Cool in pan; cut into bars. Makes 24 to 32.

Citrusy Mincemeat Squares

A flavorful bar accented by a hint of orange topped with a lemon glaze.

1/2 cup margarine or butter
1 cup brown sugar, lightly packed
1 egg
1/2 teaspoon baking soda
1-1/2 cups all-purpose flour
1/4 teaspoon ground nutmeg
3/4 cup prepared mincemeat
1/2 teaspoon grated orange peel

Glaze:
1/2 cup powdered sugar
1 teaspoon margarine or butter, room temperature
1/8 teaspoon grated lemon peel
2 to 3 teaspoons lemon juice

Preheat oven to 375F (190C). Grease a 9-inch-square baking pan. In large bowl, beat margarine, sugar and egg until fluffy. Beat in soda, flour and nutmeg. Stir in mincemeat and orange peel. Pour into prepared pan.

Bake in preheated oven 25 minutes or when top springs back when lightly touched with end of finger. Cool in pan. Drizzle with glaze. Cut into small squares. Makes 24 to 32.

Glaze:
Combine ingredients until smooth.

Hasty Blond Brownies

Especially designed for those few who do not like chocolate.

1/2 cup margarine or butter
1 cup dark-brown sugar, lightly packed
2 eggs
1 teaspoon vanilla extract
1/2 cup all-purpose flour
1/2 teaspoon baking powder
1/2 cup chopped walnuts or pecans

Preheat oven to 350F (175C). Grease an 8-inch-square pan. In medium saucepan, melt margarine with sugar. Beat in eggs, vanilla extract, flour and baking powder until well mixed. Stir in nuts.

Bake in prepared pan in preheated oven 25 to 30 minutes or until mixture begins to leave sides of pan. Cool in pan. Cut into bars or squares. Makes 20 to 25.

Tip
Save on dishwashing by using the same saucepan to melt the margarine and to combine all ingredients.

Peanut-Butter Jammies

Light jam is a reduced-calorie product usually known as a fruit spread. It is available in a variety of flavors.

2-1/2 cups all-purpose flour
3/4 cup sugar
1 egg
1/2 cup margarine or butter, room temperature
1/3 cup chunky-style peanut butter
2/3 cup light Concord grape jam

Preheat oven to 350F (175C). In large mixing bowl, combine flour, sugar, egg, margarine and peanut butter. Beat at low speed until well blended and crumbly. Remove 1-1/2 cups of crumb mixture; press remaining on bottom of an ungreased 8-inch baking pan.

Bake in preheated oven 20 to 22 minutes or until edges begin to brown. Carefully spread jam over crumb mixture in pan. Top with reserved crumbs. Return to oven 15 to 18 minutes or until light brown. Cool; cut into bars. Makes 20 to 25.

Triple-Peanut Dreams

Peanut enthusiasts think "they've died and gone to heaven" when they taste this combination.

22 graham-cracker squares
1/3 cup margarine or butter
1/4 cup peanut butter
1/2 cup brown sugar, lightly packed
1/3 cup chopped peanuts
1/2 cup peanut-butter pieces

Line cookie sheet with foil. Place graham-cracker squares on foil with edges touching. Melt margarine and peanut butter. Stir in brown sugar. Spoon over graham crackers; spread evenly. Sprinkle with peanuts and peanut-butter pieces.

Broil 5 or 6 inches from heat source 1 or 2 minutes or until bubbly. Makes 22 squares.

Refrigerate or Freeze
and Bake

Surprise your friends and offer them freshly baked cookies that you made in minutes! It's easy to perform this magic if you have a roll of "ice-box" dough in the refrigerator. These cookies were known by that name before the days of electric refrigerators. Today, we call them *refrigerator cookies*. The dough is soft at room temperature, but firm enough to slice when chilled. The dough keeps in the refrigerator for about 6 days.

Some doughs are easier to handle if they are frozen before baking. Keep them in a freezer bag in the freezer to maintain their quality until baking. Most frozen or refrigerated cookies should be sliced into 1/4-inch slices before baking. Remove and slice one roll at a time, keeping others cold or frozen until needed.

A roll of dough that begins to lose its shape while being sliced should be rotated to maintain its original shape.

Tips for freezing baked cookies
- Thoroughly cool cookies before freezing.
- Frosted cookies should be frozen uncovered until firm.
- Arrange cookies in single layers with waxed paper between layers to avoid sticking. Freeze in air-tight plastic containers or freezer bags.

Peanut-Butter 'n Honey Slices

Whip up the dough in minutes. Then freeze it and bake for impromptu special events.

1/2 cup peanut butter
1/4 cup butter-flavored vegetable shortening
1/3 cup sugar
1 egg
1/3 cup honey
1/2 teaspoon baking soda
1-3/4 cups all-purpose flour
1/2 cup chopped peanuts

In large bowl, beat peanut butter, shortening, sugar, egg, honey, soda and flour until smooth.

Form into 2 rolls about 6 x 1-1/2 inches. Wrap in plastic wrap or foil; refrigerate at least 3 hours or until firm.

Preheat oven to 375F (190C). Cut dough crosswise into 1/4-inch slices. Place about 1-inch apart on ungreased cookie sheets. Sprinkle with peanuts.

Bake in preheated oven 7 to 9 minutes or until golden. Remove from cookie sheets; cool on racks. Makes about 48.

Grandma's Butterscotch Cookies

A crispy refrigerator cookie that's been a tradition with our family for several generations.

1/2 cup vegetable shortening
1 cup brown sugar, lightly packed
1 egg
1-1/2 cups all-purpose flour
1/2 teaspoon cream of tartar
1/2 teaspoon baking soda

In medium mixing bowl, beat together all ingredients. Form into 2 rolls, 6 x 1-1/2 inches. Wrap in plastic wrap or foil; refrigerate at least 3 hours or until firm.

Preheat oven to 350F (175C). Cut chilled dough into 1/4-inch slices. Place 2 inches apart on ungreased cookie sheets.

Bake in preheated oven 9 to 11 minutes. Remove from cookie sheets; cool on racks. Makes 46 to 50 cookies.

Chill 'n Slice Molasses Cookie

Mix everything together in a saucepan to reduce dishwashing chores.

3/4 cup molasses
1/3 cup vegetable shortening
3/4 teaspoon baking soda
2 cups all-purpose flour
1 teaspoon baking powder
1 teaspoon ground ginger
1/4 teaspoon ground cloves

In medium saucepan, heat molasses to boiling point. Remove from heat. Immediately add shortening and soda; stir until shortening melts. Stir in flour, baking powder, ginger and cloves.

Cool to room temperature. Form into 2 logs of dough about 9 x 1-1/4 inches. Wrap in plastic wrap or foil; refrigerate at least 3 hours or until firm.

Preheat oven to 350F (175C). Cut dough crosswise into 1/4-inch slices. Place 1-inch apart on ungreased cookie sheets.

Bake in preheated oven 6 to 8 minutes or until firm. Remove from cookie sheets; cool on racks. Makes about 68 to 72.

Aloha Crunchies

Dried banana chips provide a wonderful fresh-tasting banana flavor with a surprisingly pleasant crunchy texture.

1 cup margarine or butter, room temperature
1 cup brown sugar, lightly packed
2-1/2 cups all-purpose flour
1/4 teaspoon baking soda
1/2 teaspoon ground mace
1 teaspoon ground cinnamon
1/4 cup dairy sour cream
1/4 cup finely chopped dried banana chips
1/2 cup finely chopped macadamia nuts

In large bowl, beat margarine and brown sugar until fluffy. Mix in flour, soda, mace, cinnamon and sour cream. Stir in dried banana chips and nuts.

Halve dough; shape each into a roll about 2 x 7 inches. Wrap in plastic wrap or foil; refrigerate at least 3 hours or until firm.

Preheat oven to 350F (175C). Cut into 1/4-inch crosswise slices. Place 2 inches apart on ungreased cookie sheets.

Bake in preheated oven 13 to 15 minutes. Remove from cookie sheets; cool on racks. Makes 45 to 48.

Chocolate Almond Slice 'n Bakes

For quick mixing use your standard-size food processor, then chill in the refrigerator for impromptu snacking.

3/4 cup toasted blanched almonds
1/2 cup margarine or butter, chilled
3/4 cup sugar
1 egg
2 (1-oz.) squares semi-sweet chocolate, melted and cooled slightly
1-1/4 teaspoons baking powder
1-1/2 cup all-purpose flour
1/4 teaspoon almond extract
3/4 cup finely chopped toasted almonds

In food processor, finely chop almonds. Remove and reserve 1/4 cup chopped almonds. Add margarine, sugar, egg, melted chocolate, baking powder, flour and almond extract. Process until well blended.

Form into one roll about 7-1/2 x 2 inches. Roll in reserve chopped almonds. Wrap in plastic wrap or foil; refrigerate at least 3 hours or until firm.

Preheat oven to 350F (175C). Cut into 1/4-inch slices. Place about 2 inches apart on cookie sheets.

Bake in preheated oven 13 to 15 minutes. Remove from cookie sheets; cool on racks. Makes 28 to 30.

Orange Slices

To pipe icing around the cookies, use 2 teaspoons orange juice in the recipe; to drizzle it with tip of spoon, add another teaspoon of juice.

1 (1/2 x 2-inch) strip orange peel
1/2 cup granulated sugar
1/3 cup butter-flavored vegetable shortening
1 egg
1/2 teaspoon baking powder
1/4 teaspoon baking soda
1-1/4 cups all-purpose flour
5 drops yellow food coloring
2 drops red food coloring

Citrus Drizzle:
1 cup powdered sugar
1 tablespoon margarine or butter, room temperature
2 to 3 teaspoons orange juice
1 teaspoon lemon juice

Remove and discard any white part from orange peel; coarsely chop. Place in food processor with granulated sugar. Process until finely minced. Add shortening, egg, baking powder, soda, flour and food coloring. Process until smooth. Form into 2 rolls about 1-1/4 x 6 inches. Wrap in plastic wrap or foil; refrigerate at least 3 hours or until firm. Preheat oven to 375F (190C). Cut into 1/4-inch crosswise slices. Place 1 inch apart on ungreased cookie sheets. Bake in preheated oven 9 to 10 minutes or until edges begin to turn golden. Remove from cookie sheets; cool on racks. Pipe Citrus Drizzle around outside edges of cooled cookie and 3 times across each. Makes 45 to 50.

Citrus Drizzle:
Beat powdered sugar, margarine, orange and lemon juice until smooth.

Superstar Frozen Chippers

Scrumptious cookies laden with two kinds of chocolate and lots of pecans.

1/2 cup margarine or butter
1/2 cup vegetable shortening
1 cup brown sugar
1/3 cup granulated sugar
2 eggs
1 tablespoon vanilla extract
1 teaspoon lemon juice
1 teaspoon baking soda
2 cups all-purpose flour
1 (12-oz.) package semi-sweet chocolate pieces
1 cup milk-chocolate pieces (about 6 oz.)
1 cup coarsely chopped pecans

In large bowl, beat all ingredients except chocolate pieces and nuts until well blended. Stir in both chocolate pieces and nuts. Using small ice-cream scoop or large kitchen spoon make 1-3/4 inch balls. Place on wax-paper-lined cookie sheet. Freeze 1 to 2 hours or until firm. Place in freezer bag; return to freezer.

A few minutes before serving time, preheat oven to 300F (150C). Place desired number about 3 inches apart on cookie sheets.

Bake in preheated oven 18 to 23 minutes, if frozen; 15 to 17 minutes, if thawed. Remove from cookie sheets; cool on racks. Makes 36.

Freeze 'n Bake Mint Sandwiches

A special addition to a holiday cookie tray or impressive treat for
St. Patrick's Day.

1 cup margarine or butter, room temperature
1/3 cup half and half
2-1/4 cups all-purpose flour
3 tablespoons granulated sugar

1-1/2 cups powdered sugar
1/4 cup melted margarine or butter
2 tablespoons milk
1/2 teaspoon mint extract
4 drops green food coloring

In medium bowl, beat 1 cup margarine, half and half and about 1 cup flour until well blended. Stir in remaining flour.

Divide in half. Form into two 6 x 1-1/2-inch rolls. Store in freezer bags. Freeze at least 4 hours or until firm.

Preheat oven to 375F (190C). Make 1/4-inch crosswise slices. Coat both sides with granulated sugar. Place on cookie sheets, prick each with fork several times.

Bake in preheated oven 8 to 10 minutes. Remove from cookie sheets; cool on racks. In small bowl, beat powdered sugar, melted margarine, milk, mint extract and food coloring. Place about 1 teaspoon of frosting on 1/2 of baked, cooled cookies. Top with remaining cookies, pressing lightly to spread frosting. Makes 24 to 26 cookie sandwiches.

Chocolate-Lovers' Ice-Cream Sandwiches

It is easy to remove one frozen sandwich at a time when you pack each in an individual plastic bag in the freezer.

1/3 cup granulated sugar
1/3 cup margarine or butter, room temperature
1 egg
1/2 teaspoon baking soda
2 cups all-purpose flour
1/2 teaspoon vanilla extract
1/2 cup thick fudge topping
1/3 cup multi-colored sprinkles
8 scoops chocolate or other flavor ice cream

Preheat oven to 350F (175C). In large bowl, beat sugar, margarine, egg, soda, flour, vanilla extract and topping.

Form into 16 balls about 1-1/2 inches in diameter. Dip tops in sprinkles and place on ungreased cookie sheet. Flatten to 3-inch diameter.

Bake in preheated oven about 10 minutes or until they are set. Remove from cookie sheet; cool on racks.

Place one scoop of ice cream on the flat side of each of 8 cookies. Press with bottom of glass or wide spatula to flatten ice cream to almost same size as cookie. Top with remaining cookies. Store in freezer in plastic bags or foil. Makes 8 sandwiches.

Freeze 'n Slice Holiday Sparkles

An unexpected pleasure lies hidden in the center.

1 (20-oz.) pkg. refrigerated sugar-cookie dough
1 (8-oz.) pkg. Neufchatel cheese, room temperature
2 tablespoons brown sugar
1/2 cup mixed candied fruits, finely chopped
1 egg white
1 tablespoon water
2 to 3 tablespoons colored sugar or nonpareils

Freeze dough. Preheat oven to 350F (175C). In small bowl, combine cheese, brown sugar and candied fruits; set aside.

Cut about one-third cookie dough into 1/8-inch rounds; return remaining dough to freezer. Spoon about 1-1/2 teaspoons cheese mixture in center of half of the cookie slices. Top each with remaining cookie slices. Lightly press edges together with fingertips to seal.

Combine egg white and water; brush on tops of filled cookies. Sprinkle with about one-third of sugar or nonpareils. Place 2 inches apart on ungreased cookie sheets.

Bake in preheated oven 10 minutes or until edges are golden. Repeat filling and baking remaining dough. Remove from cookie sheets; cool on racks. Makes 30 to 32.

Tip
When you bring the refrigerated dough home from the market, store it in your freezer. When making this recipe, you'll find it's easier to handle the dough when frozen.

Spicy Yogurt Disks

Carefully package this dough in freezer bags or wrap. Bake it when unexpected guests arrive.

1 cup margarine or butter, room temperature
1 cup brown sugar, lightly packed
2-1/2 cups all-purpose flour
1/4 teaspoon baking soda
1 teaspoon ground cinnamon
1/2 teaspoon ground ginger
1/2 teaspoon ground mace
1/4 cup plain lowfat yogurt

In large bowl, mix all ingredients until smooth. Divide dough in half. Shape each half into a 2 x 5-inch roll. Wrap each in plastic wrap or foil. Freeze at least 4 hours or overnight.

Preheat oven to 350F (175C). Cut frozen dough crosswise into 1/4-inch slices. Place 2 inches apart on ungreased cookie sheets.

Bake in preheated oven 11 to 13 minutes. Remove from cookie sheets; cool on racks. Makes 35 to 40.

Freeze 'n Bake Almond Rounds

Frozen cookie-dough log is easy to slice; do not thaw before slicing.

1/2 cup margarine or butter, room temperature
1/2 stick almond paste (3.5 oz.)
3/4 cup sugar
1 egg
1-1/2 cups all-purpose flour
2 teaspoons baking powder
1/8 teaspoon almond extract
48 to 52 whole blanched almonds

In medium mixing bowl, beat margarine and almond paste until creamy. Beat in sugar, egg, flour, baking powder and almond extract.

Form into 2 rolls about 6 x 1-1/2 inches. Wrap each in plastic wrap or foil; then in small (1 quart) plastic freezer bags. Freeze up to 2 months.

At baking time preheat oven to 375F (190C). Cut each frozen log into 1/4-inch crosswise slices. Place 2 inches apart on ungreased baking sheets. Lightly press 1 almond in center of each.

Bake in preheated oven 8 to 10 minutes or until edges are slightly browned. Remove from cookie sheets; cool on racks. Makes 48 to 52.

Red-Hot Slices

A special treat for all red-hot fans: bits and pieces throughout the cookies, plus a generous sprinkling on top.

1/2 cup red-hot candies (about 4 oz.)
1/2 cup margarine or butter
2 tablespoons sugar
1 egg
1-1/2 cups all-purpose flour
1 teaspoon baking powder

Pour red-hot candies into food processor. Turn on and off until finely chopped. Remove 3 tablespoons crushed candies; set aside. Add margarine, sugar, egg, flour and baking powder to remaining crushed candies in processor. Turn on and off until mixture is well blended. Remove from processor.

Form into a roll about 7 inches long. Wrap in plastic wrap or foil; freeze overnight.

Preheat oven to 375F (190C). Cut into crosswise slices about 1/4-inch thick. Place about 2 inches apart on ungreased cookie sheet. Sprinkle with reserved crushed red-hots.

Bake in preheated oven 9 to 11 minutes or until golden. Remove from cookie sheets immediately; cool on racks. Makes 26 to 30.

Almost-Instant Peanut-Butter Cookies

Mix and shape these cookies, then keep them in the freezer until a few minutes before you need them; bake and serve.

1/2 cup granulated sugar
1/2 cup brown sugar, lightly packed
1/2 cup margarine or butter, room temperature
1/2 cup chunky peanut butter
1 egg
1/2 teaspoon vanilla extract
1/2 teaspoon baking soda
1-2/3 cups all-purpose flour

In large bowl, combine granulated and brown sugars, margarine, peanut butter, egg and vanilla extract. Beat until well mixed. Stir in soda and flour.

Shape into 1-1/4 inch balls. Place about 2 inches apart on wax-paper-lined jelly-roll pan or cookie sheet. Flatten slightly to 1/2-inch thickness in crisscross pattern with fork tines dipped in sugar. Freeze until firm. Place in freezer bag; return to freezer.

About 20 or 30 minutes before serving time, preheat oven to 375F (190C). Remove desired number of cookies from freezer bag; return others to freezer. Place about 2 inches apart on ungreased cookie sheets.

Bake in preheated oven about 10 minutes or until set. Remove from cookie sheets; cool on racks. Makes 30 to 36 cookies.

Special-Occasion Refrigerator Mint Snaps

If you are a mint enthusiast, use the maximum amount; if not, you will enjoy these cookies with 1/2 or 3/4 teaspoon of flavoring.

1 cup margarine or butter, room temperature
1 cup powdered sugar
6 drops green food coloring
1/2 to 1 teaspoon mint flavoring
2-1/4 cups all-purpose flour
Green colored sugar
Green candied cherries, if desired

In large bowl, beat margarine, sugar, food coloring and mint flavoring until fluffy. Beat in flour.

Form into 2 rolls; each 4-1/2 x 2 inches. Roll in green sugar; wrap in plastic wrap or foil. Refrigerate at least 3 hours or until firm.

Preheat oven to 375F (190C). Remove plastic wrap or foil; cut logs crosswise into 1/4-inch slices. Place slices about 2 inches apart on ungreased cookie sheets. Top each slice with half or a quarter of a green candied cherry, if desired.

Bake in preheated oven 7 to 10 minutes. Remove from cookie sheets immediately; cool on racks. Makes 36 to 38.

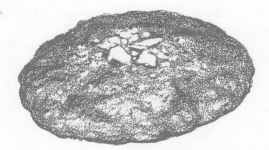

Chill 'n Bake Pistachio Slices

These pale-green cookies with pistachio flecks enhance a tray of assorted cookies for a party and taste wonderful at any occasion.

1/2 cup vegetable shortening
3/4 cup sugar
1 egg
3 drops green food coloring
1/2 teaspoon vanilla extract
1-1/2 cups all-purpose flour
1 teaspoon baking powder
1/4 cup finely chopped pistachio nuts
1 egg white, beaten slightly
1/4 cup coarsely chopped pistachio nuts

In large bowl, beat shortening, sugar, egg, food coloring and vanilla extract until well blended and fluffy. Beat in flour and baking powder. Stir in 1/4 cup finely chopped pistachio nuts.

Form into a log 2 x 7 inches long. Wrap in plastic wrap or foil; refrigerate at least 3 hours or until firm.

Preheat oven to 375F (190C). Cut dough crosswise into 1/4-inch-thick slices. Place about 2 inches apart on ungreased cookie sheets. Brush top of each slice with egg white. Then sprinkle with remaining 1/4 cup coarsely chopped pistachios.

Bake in preheated oven 9 or 10 minutes or until golden. Remove from cookie sheets; cool on racks. Makes 26 to 28.

Hazelnut Refrigerator Rounds

Grind hazelnuts in food processor or blender until consistency of fine dry bread crumbs.

1/2 cup margarine or butter, room temperature
1/2 cup powdered sugar
1/2 teaspoon vanilla extract
3/4 cup all-purpose flour
1/3 cup hazelnuts, finely ground

In medium bowl, beat margarine, sugar and vanilla extract. Beat in flour until well mixed. Stir in ground hazelnuts.

Form into 7 x 1-1/2-inch roll. Refrigerate at least 3 hours. Preheat oven to 350F (175C). Cut dough into 1/4-inch crosswise slices. Place slices 2 inches apart on ungreased cookie sheets.

Bake in preheated oven 7 to 9 minutes or until golden. Let stand 1 minute; remove from cookie sheets; cool on racks. Makes 28 to 32.